C000178854

The Crescent

Stories to introduce the concept of moral values for children aged 5 to 7

Margaret Mather and Elizabeth Yeowart

Illustrated by Philippa Drakeford

Lucky Duck is more than a publishing house and training agency. George Robinson and Barbara Maines founded the company in the 1980s when they worked together as a head and psychologist developing innovative strategies to support challenging students.

They have an international reputation for their work on bullying, self-esteem, emotional literacy and many other subjects of interest to the world of education.

George and Barbara have set up a regular news-spot on the website. Twice yearly these items will be printed as a newsletter. If you would like to go on the mailing list to receive this then please contact us:

e-mail newsletter@luckyduck.co.uk website www.luckyduck.co.uk

ISBN: 1 904 315 41 0

Published by Lucky Duck Publishing Ltd.

www.luckyduck.co.uk

Commissioning Editor: George Robinson
Editorial team: Wendy Ogden, Sarah Lynch and Mel Maines
Original artwork: Margaret Mather
Illustrator: Philippa Drakeford
Designer: Helen Weller

Printed in the UK by Antony Rowe Limited

© Margaret Mather and Elizabeth Yeowart 2004

All rights reserved. No part of this publication may be reproduced, stored in a retrieval system, or transmitted in any form, or by any means, electronic, mechanical, photocopying, recording or otherwise, without the prior, written permission of the publisher.

Rights to copy pages marked as handouts, certificates or overhead foils are extended to the purchaser of the publication for his/her use.

The right of the Author to be identified as Author of this work has been asserted by him or her in accordance with the Copyright, Design and Patents Act, 1988.

The Authors

Margaret Mather has a BA degree and a specialist qualification in fine arts. As a postgraduate she trained in Art Therapy at Goldsmiths College, London. She has been attached to child guidance clinics as part of a multi-disciplinary team and has worked on BEd courses on the therapeutic use of art. She is a member of the British Association of Art Therapists.

Elizabeth Yeowart has a BEd (hons) degree and a BSc (hons) in Psychology. She also has a post graduate diploma in Special Education (Emotional and Behavioural Difficulties) from Birmingham University and a diploma in Neuro Linguistic Programming. For many years she worked in both secondary and primary schools, latterly in an advisory capacity to teachers of emotionally and behaviourally disturbed children in junior schools. At present she is an Educational Consultant and tutors primary aged children.

Acknowledgements

The authors would like to thank Bob Yeowart and Ian Mather, Katie, Roderick and Juliet Mather, Helen Worsley, John Salter and Michael Crellin and all at Lucky Duck Publishing for their help and support. We would also like to thank Pat Whitehead for her unending enthusiasm for the project.

A note on the use of gender

Rather than repeat throughout the book the modern but cumbersome 'she/he', we have decided to use both genders equally throughout the range of activities. In no way are we suggesting a stereotype for either gender in any activity.

A note on the use of the words 'family' and 'parents'

Many children do not live in conventional two parent families. Some are looked after by the local authority and might have confusing and painful experiences. We often use the term 'carer' to identify the adults who look after such a child or young person. Sometimes 'people you live with' might be more appropriate than 'family'. These phrases can make the text rather repetitive. Please use the words most suitable for the young people you work with.

How to use the CD-ROM

The CD-ROM contains a PDF file labelled 'Worksheets.pdf' which contains worksheets for each session in this resource. You will need Acrobat Reader version 3 or higher to view and print these pages.

The document is set up to print to A4 but you can enlarge the pages to A3 by increasing the output percentage at the point of printing using the page set-up settings for your printer.

To photocopy the worksheets directly from this book, set your photocopier to enlarge by 125% and align the edge of the page to be copied against the leading edge of the copier glass (usually indicated by an arrow).

Contents

Riley Green

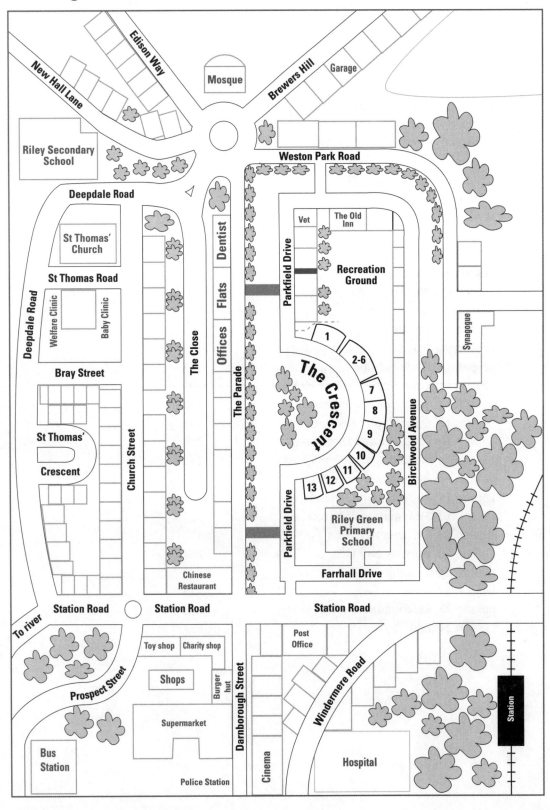

Introduction

Identifying the problem

It is generally acknowledged by teachers of the primary school aged child that there is little by way of suitable story material available for Personal Social, Health and Emotional Education. Teachers say that there are many storybooks which could be used for this subject but that they are not specifically designed for PSHE. These books are usually chosen on an ad hoc basis and consequently there is no continuity of theme or purpose. Moreover, these storybooks have to be located, read thoroughly and understood by the teacher before the message can be used and conveyed to the child. This search for suitable secular reading matter often involves a considerable amount of time.

In the past, the church saw itself as the teacher and protector of moral standards. Now, although religious leaders are prominent in expressing concern over the impact on the young of the disintegration of traditional values, concern for the moral development and emotional welfare of young children has been expressed by parents, teachers, educationalists, welfare agencies and politicians amongst others. Similarly, television programmes and articles in newspapers, journals and magazines have all raised serious questions about the attitude and responsibilities of society towards young children. The old system has changed and now nobody seems to know who is in charge. Most feel that the schoolteacher and parents should be responsible for moral teaching and believe that 'they should do it'. We take the view that at present there is a lack of suitable secular reading matter, and that primary school teachers and parents suffer from a lack of teaching aids with a moral content. But what kind of aid do we propose?

What we propose

We feel that one of the most effective ways of capturing the attention of the child and of introducing the concept of moral values is by means of 'the story'. All children love stories. The stories of The Crescent are designed to be read to the child and are intended to act as a trigger or starting point for further work and discussion. The storyline is intended to act as a 'mini soap-opera' for children. Children will identify with the characters of The Crescent and will be familiar with their daily activities, relationships, emotions, hopes and fears. The programme is designed in such a way as to allow the child to form his or her own opinions as to the 'right or wrong' in the story which will be based on the child's own experiences.

The child should be given enough time to think or reflect on any other associated ideas and the parent or teacher may find that sometimes days later reference is made to the theme of the story or its content. A non-judgemental approach together with time to play with ideas is essential for a child's emotional growth and moral welfare. A child must experience and experiment to gain understanding of its own inner and outer worlds. By identifying and empathising with the characters and situations in the stories it is hoped that children will be given the opportunity to work on emotional and moral issues. Our obligation to the child is to provide the safety and structure for this opportunity:

- Anecdotal tales from The Crescent attempt to deal with themes which are common to all. In so doing they should be as relevant for the child brought up in the inner city as the one who lives in a more rural or suburban environment.

- By using realistically based stories or short anecdotal tales, the child should be able to identify with the situations created and through questioning, extract meaning through the parable. The use of open questions helps the child to deliver more than a 'yes' or 'no' answer, and develop understanding and empathy. Worksheets including Circle Time discussion are used to develop this aim and are part of the lesson activities provided.

- Each story could be an opportunity for children to express their own thoughts and provide them with a vehicle for voicing their own feelings.

- The Crescent stories might enable them to share their findings with others and realise that they are not alone in their fears, hopes and questionings. The stories and subsequent work encourage empathy.

- The stories' messages could provide children with an opportunity to think for themselves about what is 'right' or 'wrong' and help them to form their own judgements. A young child needs to know why something is 'good' or 'bad' and needs to find an explanation. Rules, orders and dictates are simply not good enough for a young child's enquiring mind. Feelings and emotions are not changed or helped by orders. Dwivedi and Gupta (2000) when talking about issues like violence, loss and bullying, say, "There is an urgent need to devise programmes which go to the roots of problems."

● The stories are not doctrinaire but are written with multicultural, economic and environmental awareness issues in mind; citizenship, empathy, confidence and responsibility are promoted as is the development of good relationships and respect for others.

● The stories have strong connections with other subjects, in particular, English Speaking and Listening, Geography and Art and Design.

The Crescent is a programme in three volumes written for three different age levels: Infants, Lower Junior and Upper Junior. This volume is for infants at Key Stage I and contains stories designed to be read to the child. Ideas for discussion, illustrations and work-sheets with teacher's notes and guidelines accompany the stories. Tales from The Crescent could be used in Circle Time or assembly as well as the timetable for PSHE and other linking subjects. But it is important to note that the classroom should not be considered the sole domain for these stories; they will be of interest to parents, carers, playgroup leaders and all those who work closely with young children. Although the book is written with instructions for the children to 'sit in a circle' this is a suggestion only; other methods or situations may be used which are more appropriate in individual schools.

The advantages of our stories

In general, stories provide opportunities for children's imagination to work. Imagination is a key aspect to moral development. The 'let's pretend' and 'as if' provides the child with opportunities to express feelings. The child often uses 'mask' or 'persona' as a vehicle to express feelings and this allows access for personal expression. It is the freedom afforded to the child through work and play that is ben-eficial and which the child feels as non-threatening. The children might, for example, make their own puppets, draw and paint or talk and enact the story lines. As well as the suggestions in this book the teacher will have ideas of her own. This will help to reinforce the message as well as providing children with some autonomy and opportunity to form their own interpretations and share them with others. "Children need respect and acknowledgement of their experiences" (Monroe and Kraus, (2000).

Playing with ideas and mental image making processes allows a child to bridge the gap between play and reality. These are important lessons in early years and through work and play the child begins to grasp the notion of 'self and others' and to distinguish between its own needs and the other person's needs. By reading the stories from The Crescent, by playing with the ideas and by being encouraged to share findings a young child should discover that home, school and the community at large is affected by the actions and attitudes of its members. "Schools are one of our last hopes for rescuing and reinventing community" (Bovair, 2000). The child should also begin to grasp how actions can have positive and negative consequences depending on whether those actions are constructive or destructive. (These points are illustrated in the stories from The Crescent and the child should be able to extract these messages and refer them to its own world. This is helped by the questions derived in Circle Time discussion.) The voice of the character will also assist the child in making comparisons and to examine its own experiences.

Feelings of self-worth are important and children who are encouraged to appreciate their own intrinsic value are less likely to tolerate discrimination and unfairness. They are also more able to take a stand against injustice and prejudice. They are stronger in resisting peer group pressure if they know it to be wrong. Because prejudices and stereotypes are not so firmly ingrained in the younger child's mind, and in early years children are more flexible and open to influences, they do not have the tendency to hide their feelings like older children. They are more 'up-front' and more willing to name their likes and dislikes. The young child is usually uninhibited in saying what is 'good' and what is 'bad'.

Environmental issues are also important and included, as are informed choices. The lessons identify those who might help us, such as families, friends, neighbours, doctors and teachers, and how to ask for help.

All people in The Crescent are valued regardless of race, creed, ability or disability and gender.

The Crescent deals with emotional life, the strength of our emotions and impulses and how we identify them. It has long been argued that "the interactions of life's earliest years lay down a set of emotional lessons based on the attainments and upsets" (Goleman, 2000) between care givers and infants.

Wolfendale (2000) emphasises the importance of early years' education and notes the importance of intervention of early appearing needs. These can be 'potent' and 'chaotic' (Goleman 2000). Emotional difficulties in the personal lives of children can have a massive impact on cognitive ability (Goleman 2000 and Greenwood 2000). It is because of this that the authors consider this work with the infant child to be of significant importance and should be addressed. This book goes part way towards that end.

Chapter 1

Setting the Scene

This is a group of stories, thematic in nature, based on a small community living in The Crescent. It is written with the PSHE curriculum in mind although it has many links with other areas of the curriculum. These are dealt with later.

The stories for infants take place at home, school, on the local recreation ground, at the local cinema and shops in town including the burger bar. This reflects the world of the young child. The Crescent characterises the people important to the child, that is to say parents, siblings, friends, neighbours, school friends and the teacher.

The Crescent covers differences in gender, culture and race, position in family, ability and disability; its aim is to encourage good citizenship. The characters for infants are a collection of unique individuals who share similarities and differences. It is democracy where each member has a voice. In this way The Crescent heeds the voice of Bovair (2000) who argues, "education is essential for democracy". The main characters for the infant stories and their houses in The Crescent are listed below:

Number 8

Leroy and Linda are four years old. They are twins. They are the main characters of these stories. They live with their mum, Brenda, and their dad, Josh, and half sister Jenny, who is eleven years old. They are both friends and rivals but care deeply for each other, families, friends and neighbours.

Brenda is Leroy, Linda and Jenny's mother. She works as an assistant warden at Morningdale Court, which is sheltered accommodation for the disabled.

Josh is dad to Leroy and Linda, and a very good step dad to Jenny. Josh's parents are from Barbados in the West Indies but Josh was born in Britain. He went to school and then to music college where he met his wife, Brenda. Now he works as a music lecturer and has a window cleaning round. There is very little of a practical nature that Josh cannot turn his hand to. He is versatile and creative. He finds he can compose his music when cleaning windows.

Jenny is the twins' half sister. She is eleven years old and is in Year 6 at school. She has a good relationship with all her family but sometimes finds the twins a nuisance. Her birth father is absent and something of a mystery at this stage.

Number 7

Paul Brownlow is six years old. He is next door neighbour to Leroy and Linda and sometimes he plays with the twins. He is especially fond of his truck, a transitional object. He misses his mum, Sylvia, who is in hospital as a long-term patient.

Stephen Brownlow is Paul's dad. He is a builder and he runs his own business.

Matti Brownlow is Paul's grandmother and lives with Paul and his dad whilst mum is in hospital.

Morningdale Court Number 2 - 6

Ronnie Calderbank is sixty years old. He lives at Morningdale Court, The Crescent. He uses a wheelchair and is a cheerful character. Eventually Ronnie and Matti get married.

Sophie Sellars also lives at Morningdale Court. Sometimes she is the storyteller to the children in The Crescent and she is blind. She has a guide dog, Hope.

Number 1

Sali, Tim and baby Zoë Romanov live at No. 1, The Crescent. Sali helps at the corner shop whilst Tim, Zoë's dad, is a travel agent in the town.

Number 13

Mr Alsop, often called Mr Allsorts because he sells everything, owns the corner shop. He keeps his shop in good order and is interested in the daily happenings of The Crescent.

Number 12

Dr. Benson has a surgery, but does not live, at No. 12, The Crescent. He has a partner (who is introduced later in the junior stories), and a nurse. He also has a small ailments/baby clinic upstairs.

Number 9

Shama is a student studying veterinary medicine. She lives at No. 9, The Crescent. She has a dog called Frisky. Two other students share the house. They are Marcus who studies Maths and Stuart who studies Ecology.

Number 10

Susie is ten years old. She often visits her grandfather and grandmother, Mary and Gerald, who live at No. 10 and dote on her. She enjoys many privileges like music and swimming lessons, she has many treats and a high level of spending money from parents and grandparents.

Number 11

This is the Mystery House. Its doors and windows are boarded up and no one lives there.

The Crescent houses a collection of unique individuals who share similarities but also differences. Each respects the other, which makes for a democratic community. Occasionally they call a residents' meeting to discuss concerns.

Chapter 2

Themes and Objectives

The lessons, which are linked to a month of the year, consist of:

- A preparatory 'warm up' exercise before listening to the story.

- A story from The Crescent based on a theme.

- Notes of suggested ideas for the teacher including Circle Time discussion and ideas to link the story with other areas of the curriculum.

- One or two worksheets that can be photocopied for use by the child.

Themes, aims and objectives, a synopsis of the story and national curriculum links are outlined in the lesson notes.

The themes of Infant Stories from The Crescent and the month and number to which they belong can be seen in the following table, Themes and Stories. It must be noted that although the infant stories are allocated a number and a month of the year this is not prescriptive and the thematic stories can be used in a different order to reflect the needs of the school, teacher or child. However some of the stories reflect the season of the year to which they are allocated. Although the stories can be read in any order it is suggested that the 'Introduction to The Crescent', which takes the form of the story 'The Letter Game', should be read first.

Where extra sensitive issues are developed an animal mouthpiece is used in the stories. Thus a goose is employed to illustrate the concept of bullying (April) and a fox is used to illustrate 'stranger danger' (April). Themes and stories are listed together with lesson links to other areas of the curriculum, in the second table, Objectives.

Themes and Stories

Month and Story No.		Theme	Title of story
Aug	1	Introduction	The Letter Game
	2	New Beginnings	The New Beginning
Sept	3	Assumption and Prejudice	The Ambulance Man's Daughter
	4	Territory and Trespass	The 'Not About Us' Story
Oct	5	Vandalism	The Paper Crown
	6	The Countryside	The Mallard
Nov	7	Giving and Taking	The Teddy Bears' Picnic
	8	The Unknown	The Monster
Dec	9	Play and Creativity	The Christmas Cards
	10	Darkness and Light	The Glow in the Dark
Jan	11	Loss, Rejection and Identification	The Sad Happening
	12	Thoughts and Promises	The Guinea Pigs
Feb	13	Disaster and Recovery	The Accident
	14	Laughter and Derision	The Laugh
March	15	Weddings and Formalities	The Wedding
	16	Birth and New Arrivals	The Surprise
April	17	Bullying and Friendship	The Goose
	18	Strangers and Danger	The Young Fox
May	19	Excitement	The Exciting Day
	20	Honesty and Lies	The Little Black Kitten
June	21	Stealing	The Mystery Thief
	22	Guilt	The Plums
July	23	Restoration and Discovery	The Goldfish
	24	Endings	The Plan

Objectives

Lesson	Theme and Story	Objectives
1	**Introduction** The Letter Game.	PSHE 1a,b,c. 2a, f, e. 3g. 4b,c, d. 5f. English 1. 1a, b, c. 2a, c, d. 3a, c. English 2. 1b. English 3. 4a, e. Science 2. 4a. Art & Design 2a.
2	**New Beginnings** The New Beginning.	PSHE 1a,b,c. 2a, c, e. 3d. 4c. English 1. 1a, b, c. 2a, c, d. 3a, c. Mathematics 2. 2a.
3	**Assumption and Prejudice** The Ambulance Man's Daughter.	PSHE 1c. 2a. 3g. 4c, d, e. 5b. English 1. 1a, b, c. 2a, c, d. 3a, c.
4	**Territory and Trespass** The 'Not About Us' Story.	PSHE 1a, b. 2a, e. 3a. 4d. 5b. English 1. 1a, b, c. 2a, c, d. 3a, c.
5	**Vandalism** The Paper Crown.	PSHE 1a, b, c. 2a, c, e, f, h. 3e. 4a, b, d, 5f, g. English 1. 1a, b, c. 2a, c, d. 3a, c. Art & Design 2c. 5a.
6	**The Countryside** The Mallard.	PSHE 1a, b, d. 2a, c, e, g. 3a, g. 4c. English 1. 1a, b, c. 2a, c, d. 3a, b, c. English 2. 1f. 2a. 6a, b. Geography. 1a, c. Art & Design. 2a. 4a.
7	**Giving and Taking** The Teddy Bears' Picnic	PSHE 1a, c. 2a, c, f. 3d. 4a, c, d. 5e, f. English 1. 1a, b, c. 2a. 3a, b. 9a, b. Art & Design. 2c.
8	**The Unknown** The Monster.	PSHE 1a, b, c, d. 2a, g. 3g. English 1. 1a, b, c. 2a, c, d. 3a, c. English 3.12 Art & Design. 1a.
9	**Play and Creativity** The Christmas Cards.	PSHE 1a, b, c, d. 2a, e. 3f. 4b, d, e. 5f English 1. 1a, b, c. 2a, c, d. 3a, c. Art & Design. 1a.
10	**Darkness and Light** The Glow in the Dark.	PSHE 1a, c, d. 2a, e. 3g. 4a, b, c, d, e. 5b, e. English 1. 1a, b, c. 2a, c, d. 3a, c. Art & Design. 5c.

11	**Loss, Rejection and Identification** The Sad Happening.	PSHE 1b, c. 2a, e, f. 4d. English 1. 1a, b, c. 2a, c, d. 3a, e. English 2. 1f.
12	**Thoughts and Promises** The Guinea Pigs.	PSHE 1a, b. 2a, c, d, e. 3f. 4c, d, e. 5e, f. English 1. 1a, b, c. 2a, c, d. 3a, c. English 2. 1f. Science 2. 1a. 2b, e.
13	**Disaster and Recovery** The Accident.	PSHE 1a, b. 2a, e, f. 3a, g. 4a, d. English 1. 1a, b, c. 2a, c, d. 3a, c. Science 3. 1a.
14	**Laughter and Derision** The Laugh.	PSHE 1c. 2a, f. 4d. 5b. English 1. 1a, b, c. 2a, c, d. 3a, c.
15	**Weddings and Formalities** The Wedding.	PSHE 1a, c. 2a, c, f, i. 4d. English 1. 1a, b, c. 2a, c, d. 3a, c. English 2. 1i. Art & Design. 1a.
16	**Birth and New Arrivals** The Surprise.	PSHE 1a, d. 2a, e, f. 3d. 4c. 5c. English 1. 1a, b, c. 2a, c, d. 3a, c. ·English 3. 4b, d, e. Science 2. 1b.
17	**Bullying and Friendship** The Goose.	PSHE 1a. 2a. 4a, d, e. 5g. English 1. 1a, b, c. 2a, c, d. 3a, c. PE 1a.
18	**Strangers and Danger** The Young Fox.	PSHE 1c. 2a, f. 3g. 4d. English 1. 1a, b, c. 2a, c, d. 3a, c. 9b.
19	**Excitement** The Exciting Day.	PSHE 1b, c. 2a, c, f, g, i. 3g. 4c, d. 5b. English 1. 1a, b, c. 2a, c, d. 3a, c. 4a, b. English 3. 1c. 4e. Geography. 1c.
20	**Honesty and Lies** The Little Black Kitten.	PSHE 1a. 2a. 4a, d. English 1. 1a, b, c. 2a, c, d. 3a, c. Art & Design. 5c.
21	**Stealing** The Mystery Thief.	PSHE 1a, b, c. 2a, c, f. 4a. 5a, f. English 1. 1a, b, c. 2a, c, d. 3a, c.

22	**Guilt** The Plums.	PSHE 1a, b, c. 2a, c. 3f. 4d. English 1. 1a, b, c. 2a, c, d. 3a, c. Mathematics. 1f. Science 2. 1a. Art & Design. 1a.
23	**Restoration and Recovery** The Goldfish.	PSHE 1a, e. 2a, e. 3b. 4d. 5a, b. English 1. 1b, c. 2a, c, d. 3a, c. English 3. 1d. Science 2. 1a.
24	**Endings** The Plan.	PSHE 1a, b, c. 2a, f. 3g. 4a. English 1. 1a, b, c. 2a, c, d. 3a, c.

Chapter 3

How to Use the Materials

We have included some ideas on how the materials may be used. This is not an exhaustive or rigid list. The Crescent is a diverse programme and "diversity demands flexibility". (Bovair 2000). Equally, the book does not demand expensive resources but urges the teacher to know about the materials they have and use them well.

- The stories were designed to be read by an adult to the child rather than by the child.

- The stories can be read in assembly with follow-up work in assembly or in the classroom. They can be read as part of PSHE time or they can be linked to other areas of the curriculum.

- Stories and worksheets can be differentiated to suit the needs of the individual child or group of children.

- The scheme can be used in the construction and implementation of Individual Education Plans and should be adapted where necessary.

- Worksheets and teacher's notes can be used at both an individual and group level. Teachers should build on the strengths of the children.

- By valuing all children the teacher will set the climate for empathy and consideration of another perspective.

- Especially the withdrawn child should feel safe in a non-critical environment. Puppets or a mouthpiece could be used to foster confidence in the withdrawn child.

- In understanding and celebrating uniqueness the teacher should value differences between individuals regardless of race, culture, gender, ethnicity, belief, ability or disability.

- With the child's help, ground rules of no criticism and co-operation should be encouraged. Children can be reminded of their own rules. Rogers (2000) encourages teachers to "refer again to the class rules... in our classroom".

- Circle Time is used in different ways by different people. In this publication the questions for discussion can best be dealt with by all teachers, helpers and children sitting in a large circle, which could contain a whole class or a smaller group. The circle shape maximises a feeling of acceptance and safety and symbolises unity and containment. The following rules are suggested:

Only one person speaks at any one time. In Circle Time for young children a tangible or 'speaking' object is held by the speaker and no one speaks except that person. This object can be a shell, a puppet or a soft toy. We have used a 'talking bird' puppet. This can be used to help the withdrawn child to speak, by the teacher asking the child if the 'talking bird' wants to say something even if the child doesn't wish to speak. In this way the puppet is not only used as a 'speaking object' but also a mouthpiece. No one speaks if they do not want to nor does one person humiliate another. However, the children who do not wish to speak first time round can be given a second chance. The teacher might say something like 'I wonder if the talking bird wants to tell us something now'. (See the template on page 26.)

This template is of a 'talking bird'. It can be used for each child to colour in or it can be adapted and made into a glove puppet with the fingers to be placed in the upper beak and the thumb in the lower beak. It can also be made into a symbol, which can show that The Crescent work is about to begin, and placed in a prominent position in the classroom or hall. To make The Crescent moon bird into a symbol the teacher needs white card and a lollipop stick. Using the template the teacher should trace and cut out two crescent moon birds. She will then colour the birds emphasising the crescent shaped wings and the crescent shape in the bird's eyes. The two cardboard cut outs can then be stuck together with a lollipop stick set in between the cardboard cut outs. It would be advantageous and consistent if the moon bird was displayed when each 'Crescent' story, lesson and worksheet is being used.

- All children should be encouraged by the teacher to speak audibly.

- All children should be helped where necessary to structure their thoughts so that they convey what they mean to say to others.

- The teacher can mirror the child's utterances or re-word where meaning is unclear. The use, by the teacher, of the words "could it be that" may be useful here (Long 2000). We could paraphrase, reflect feelings, summarise and focus. This will help to develop empathy and show unconditional acceptance. We have also found the use of the word 'perhaps' encourages the child to describe feelings. For example the teacher could say, "Perhaps you think that Becky knew some facts that the other children did not know". Alternatively it could be said by the teacher, "Could it be that Becky knew some facts that the other children did not know? Do you think there was something that Becky was worried about saying?"

- Teachers should understand that the nature of the child's disclosure may lead to sensitive issues being raised. Thoughtful, receptive, accepting and sympathetic responses are advocated.

- Above all do not worry about fostering co-operation in a competitive world. In the world as it is the child will develop coping strategies. Within the setting and safety of The Crescent expressions of feeling and empathy are encouraged.

- To contain the children's work on The Crescent a folder should be made by the teacher or helper or be bought by the school. The folder will enable each child to store his/her worksheets and colouring in sheets which can be found in this book.

- The teacher should give each child a copy of the picture on page 27 and tell them that later they will colour in the picture and make the figure in the picture look like themselves 'dressing' the figure with for example, a dress, a skirt, trousers, a sari, shorts, a jumper or a scarf. When they have finished the picture they should add their name and class. The teacher or helper may have to supply a model from which they can copy their name or in some cases write the name for the child.

When each child has finished his drawing the teacher or helper should glue the picture onto the folder which has already been made.

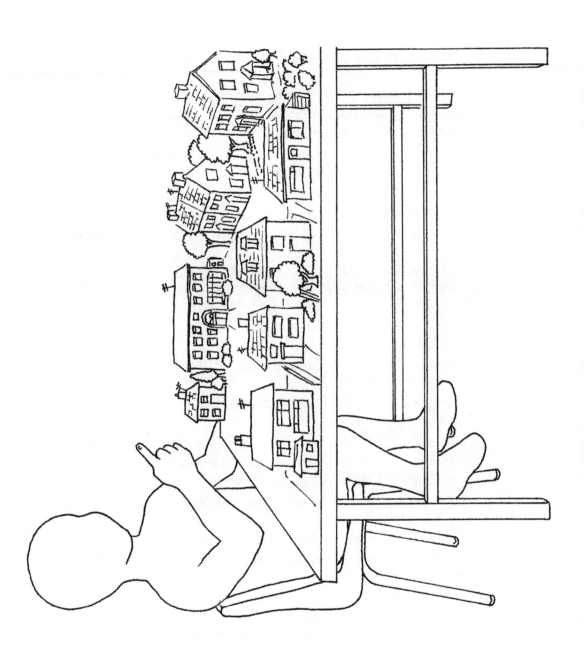

Bibliography

Axline, V. M. (1964) *Dibbs in Search of Self*. Penguin Books, London.

Axline, V. M. (1969) *Play Therapy*. Ballantine Books, New York.

Bennet, M., ed. (1993) *The Child as Psychologist*. Harvester Wheatsheaf, Hemel Hempstead.

Bovair, K. (2000) Building a New Future. *Special!* Spring 2000, Hobsons (NASEN). Cambridge.

Collins, M. (2001) *Because We're Worth It*. Lucky Duck Publishing Ltd., Bristol.

Collins, M. (2002) *Because I'm Special*. Lucky Duck Publishing Ltd., Bristol.

Dwivedi, K. N. and Gupta, A. (2000) Keeping Cool: anger management through group work. *Support for Learning*, May 2000. NASEN. Tamworth.

DfEE. (1999) *The National Curriculum*. The Stationery Office, London.

Goleman, D. (1996) *Emotional Intelligence*. Bloomsbury Publishing Plc., London.

Greenwood, A. (2001) Losses and Numbers. *Special!* Summer 2001. Hobsons (NASEN) Cambridge.

Long, R. (2000) *Facing Lions*. Rob Long's Education Works. Totnes.

Monroe, B. and Kraus, F. (2000) Coping with Death. *Special!* Autumn 2000. Hobsons (NASEN) Cambridge.

Moseley, J. (1996) *Quality Circle Time in the Primary Classroom*. L.D.A., Wisbech.

Rae, T. (2000) *Purr-Fect Skills*. Lucky Duck Publishing Ltd., Bristol

Rogers, B. (2000) Time to Reflect. *Special!* Spring 2000. Hobsons (NASEN) Cambridge.

Sharp, S. and Smith, P. K. (eds) (1994) *Tackling Bullying in Your School*. Routledge, London.

Wolfendale, S. (2000) Special Needs in the early years: prospects for policy and practice. *Support for Learning*. November 2000, NASEN, Tamworth.

Chapter 4

The Lessons

Lesson 1: August

Story: The Letter Game
Theme: Introduction to The Crescent

The characters and illustrations are introduced to the children. Friendships and neighbourliness are important. The people of The Crescent organise a street party and Leroy and Linda match initial letters to characters.

Objectives

- To recognise what the children like and dislike.

- To share their opinions on things that matter to them and explain their views.

- To recognise and name their feelings.

- To take part in discussions.

- To understand that they belong to communities.

- To realise that people have needs.

- To understand some ways of keeping safe.

- To play and work co-operatively and develop relationships through work.

- To identify some differences between people.

- To know that family, friends and neighbours should care for each other.

Preparing for the story

Play 'The Letter Game'

The children, teacher and helpers sit in a circle. The teacher says to the children, "I am thinking of the name of someone in this class and their name begins with the letter P. Put up your hands if you think you know the answer." The teacher chooses a child whose hand is raised. The child gives the name 'Paula'.

PSHE
4b.

English 1.
1a, 2a.

English 2
1b.

The teacher replies, "Yes that is correct, I was thinking of the name Paula", or "You are right that Paula begins with a letter P but I was thinking of someone else, would anyone else like to think of another name?"

The teacher chooses another child who gives the name 'Peter'. The teacher replies, "Yes that is correct, I was thinking of Peter." The teacher then thinks of the name of another child beginning with a different letter or another helper or a child might take a turn to 'become teacher'.

Read the story

After the above activity has been completed the teacher reads the story to the children.

It will be seen that in the story the letter game is played by the children of The Crescent. This indirectly introduces them to the characters in the stories.

Circle Time Discussion

The Circle Time discussion points can be conducted in the following way. The children, teacher and helpers sit in one large circle. A speaking object or mouthpiece is produced, for example, a shell, a small model or soft toy or the talking bird.

The teacher could say:

> "This speaking object or mouthpiece will be passed round the circle. You will have a chance to say something about the questions that we are discussing only when it is passed to you. Everyone will have a turn to speak and we will all get many chances to listen. You do not have to speak. If you do not wish to say anything pass your speaking object or mouthpiece to the next person on your left. The first question is…
>
> I will say what I think first and then I will pass the speaking object to John. You can smile or not. Remember to watch John carefully, watching his face, his expression and the way he sits. How are his arms and legs placed? Does he look happy, angry or sad? After John has spoken the speaking object is passed to the next person on his left, but before he does this I will say something to John (see Note). Everyone will have a turn to tell us what they think and we will know that what they say

is important. We will show that we think that what everybody says is important by listening very, very, carefully."

Note

This would be the time when the teacher can clarify what he or she thinks the child is saying. As stated in the introduction the child's words can be paraphrased and used in a clearer way, probably introduced by the words 'could it be' or 'perhaps'. For example: "Could it be that you think Tom is the same as you because you both have blonde hair, but different from you because he is a boy and you are a girl", or "Perhaps you think that Carol might like to be introduced politely to other people because she is a new girl to our school."

During Circle Time the teacher encourages speaking skills, helping the child to speak with clear diction and appropriate intonation, choosing words with precision and organising what they say.

At the same time the teacher should remind the listening child to sustain concentration and listen to other children's reactions. They should be encouraged by the teacher to remember specific points that interest them and, when it is their turn to speak, to keep their comments relevant to what has gone on before remembering the views of other speakers. Children, using the talking object, will take turns in speaking.

Questions

Before looking at each question individually it is useful for the teacher to consider how the questions are asked, and to prompt for additional information from the child. The child may need help in forming his or her opinions. In each Circle Time discussion the aim is to hear and value the children's point of view; a scaffold is provided for the child's own ideas and concepts. For each Circle Time discussion question there are some questions as notes for teachers.

Question 1. Is everyone the same or different?

Do we all have some things which are the same or different from other people? Do we all look alike? Are we the same gender as some people and a different gender from some other people? Do we all have the same physical characteristics? Do we all have the same eye colour or hair colour? Do we all do certain things the same? For example, do all living things breathe; do we all drink milk, water or Coca Cola? Do we all have the same hobbies or pastimes? Do we all

PSHE
2a, 4c.

English 1.
1a, b, c. 2a, c, d. 3a, c.

Science 2.
4a.

33

like the same things? Do we all need shelter? Do we all need love and affection in order to grow?

Question 2. In which ways would you like to be introduced?

PSHE
1a. 2a.

English 1.
1a, b, c. 2a, c, d.
3a, c.

What the child likes will be specific to him or her. Most children seem to like something which adds information about them and which they find complimentary. For example "This is Tom, he is good at football, he has just come from another school", or "This is Becky, I'm sitting near her in class because she is kind and lends me her crayons." Some introductions could include sharing, being kind, knowing and understanding jokes and having a good sense of humour, having likes, for example sport or computers and being interested in other people.

Question 3. Who lives in your street?

PSHE
1a. 2f. 3g.

English 1.
1a, b, c. 2a, c, d.
3a, c.

Here the child's neighbours are explored: their characters, idiosyncrasies, possessions, in fact anything which tells us what they are like. What is their gender, race, creed or age? Are they disabled in any way? Do the children know everybody or just some people? Do any of the people they know have anything that is special to them? Do they like or dislike any of their neighbours? Do you care for your neighbours? Do any of the children have neighbours in the caring professions: teachers, dinner ladies, traffic wardens, lollipop ladies, policemen, nurses, doctors etc.? Do these people help us to keep safe?

Question 4. Who were friends in the story of The Crescent? Is it nice to have friends?

PSHE
2a, 4d.

English 1.
1a, b, c. 2a, c, d.
3a, c.

This question asks for certain knowledge. Appropriate answers could be Leroy, Linda and Paul, Jenny and Susie, Brenda and the residents of Morningdale Court, Ronnie and Sophie and Hope her guide dog. It could be said that all the residents of The Crescent are friends one with another. The people of The Crescent had a party and shared their food and drink. Is sharing a good thing to do?

Question 5. What makes a good friend?

What sort of greeting can be associated with a good friend? What do good friends say? The teacher gives an example. Is everyone the same kind of friend? Do good friends share? Do good friends include you in their games? Do good friends play with you? Do you talk and laugh with your friends? Is it important that you like the same things? Do good friends go to each other's houses? Are neighbours sometimes good friends? Do you share secrets with a good friend? Do good friends always get on with each other or do they sometimes quarrel? Does a good friend know how to 'make up?' Do good friends ask advice of each other? Do good friends smile or laugh all the time or are they sometimes sad? Are there times when you feel the same thing as a good friend? For example, if they have fallen and hurt their knee do you feel a little bit sad for them? Do you try to comfort good friends if they are sad for any reason? If a good friend has happy news are you pleased for them?

PSHE
1a, b. 2a, e. 4d.

English 1.
1a, b, c. 2a, c, d.
3a, c.

Question 6. How would you feel if you had no friends?

Would you feel sad and want to cry, or would you be happy and pleased if you had no friends? What would you miss most if you had no friends? Would it be easy to comfort another or share an interest? Whose house would you go to if you had no friends? What might someone say to you if they were not going to be your friend? (This is a very sensitive issue and should be handled with great care; the teacher may not want to include this in discussion time.

PSHE
1a, b, c. 2a.

English 1.
1a, b, c. 2a, c, d.
3a, c.

Supplementary ideas

The children work in groups of four in their classroom but each child is given a partner. Each child is also given a self-adhesive label. (The large ones are best for the younger child.) The children are asked to decorate their label or badge in their own way. They may draw a pattern, or a picture of their own choice: perhaps something they like doing such as skipping or playing football. The children write either their own name or the initial of their first name. The children then put their badges in the middle of the table and then they must establish which badge belongs to which person. When this is established the children wear their badges. Each child must then say one affirmative thing about their partner.

PSHE
1a. 5f.

English 3.
4a, e.

The children work in pairs. All children will have an opportunity to draw or to paint or make a clay model of their partner. The children will work from direct observation of their partner who will act as model for the likeness to be painted, drawn or modelled. The children then return to their seats. The teacher asks for volunteers to show what they have created. Each child who has volunteered introduces the friend that acted as a model to the class and then displays their creation to the class. The child thinks of one way that the representation is similar to them and one way in which it is dif-

PSHE
4c.

English I.
1a, 2a.

ferent. For example, Amy is wearing red shoes and I am wearing red shoes (same). Amy has blonde hair and I have brown hair (different). The class then think of other ways that are not necessarily represented by the picture that Amy and her friend are the same or different. For example, Amy likes to go to Brownies but Jo likes football). Encourage the children to speak with clear diction and listen carefully.

PSHE
5f.

Art and
Design
2a.

The teacher reminds the children that the people of The Crescent organised a party together; to do this they were co-operative and friendly. The teacher tells the children that they are all going to make an individual item to use in a big co-operative venture. Each child will make a model of a house where a character lived; ready made boxes should be used that can be decorated by painting them a brick colour or a pebble-dashed or rendered colour. Windows and doors could be added from pieces of collage material, as can curtains, drainpipes and window boxes etc. Before beginning the task the teacher should discuss with the class what characteristics their house will have. When each child has made a house the teacher collects the individual boxes and makes a crescent shape of the houses. The caption could read 'We made a Crescent together'.

The children sit in a large circle on the floor. The teacher asks the children if they think that the people of The Crescent knew something about each other before they had the party. Did they know each other's names and where they lived? Might they talk with each other at the party to find out more about each other? Here are some of the things they might have asked:

PSHE
1b. 5f.

English I.
1a, 2a.

What were their likes and dislikes? What do they do in their leisure time? Did anyone have interesting hobbies? Where did they like to go? Did they go to the cinema, the theatre, the burger bar, restaurant or cafes? Did they like science, the countryside, animals, birds and minibeasts? Did they ever go to the recreation ground alone or was it safer to go with others, who they knew well? Why was that? Did they own a special object or teddy bear, toy or truck, collection of coins or stamps etc? The children are helped to form two circles, an inner and an outer circle with equal numbers in each circle.

Each child will find they have a partner. Their task is to interview their partner. (The teacher can give some of the examples above to the children.) When the children have finished the interview (say five minutes) all children come back into a large circle. It is now that each child can tell the class something about their partner. The children, who are wearing the introductory badges that they have made, all share a piece of fruit, biscuits and a drink. (The children could have contributed something to 'the party'. It should be emphasised that this is a time to share.)

Instructions for the worksheet

"Jenny has made some letters for Leroy and Linda. On the worksheet you will see some letter 'L's. Can you find them? This is the initial or first letter for 'Linda' and the initial or first letter for 'Leroy'. There is also a 'J' for 'Jenny'. Can you see a 'J' in the picture? The children are taking some jelly to the party. Jenny explained to Leroy and Linda that if there was an 'E' and a 'Y' in the picture the letter would spell 'jelly'. You can see a pattern at the bottom of the page marked with 'J's and 'L's. Can you make a repeating pattern from your own initials and a friend's initials? If your name is 'Sali' and your friend's name is 'Thomas' you could write a pattern by writing first an 'S' and then a 'T'. You could repeat this across the page from beginning to end just like Jenny did with L and J. When you have done this you can colour the picture and the pattern. Remember to make your pattern like Jenny's pattern but use your own initial and a friends."

The Letter Game

"Guess which person I'm thinking of," said Leroy to his twin sister, Linda.

They were playing a game.

"You have to tell me what letter their name begins with," answered Linda.

"It begins with a letter P," Leroy replied.

"Well, is it the Postman?"

"No!" Leroy laughed.

Linda thought hard.

"I know. I know. It's Paul," and she laughed too.

She was right.

Paul is the boy who lives next door.

"Now it's my turn," said Linda. "The person I am thinking about has a name that begins with 'R'."

Leroy tried to guess. He was wondering who it could be.

At that moment their daddy came into the room. He said he would help Leroy to guess.

"I don't think it's a boy or a girl," said Josh.

Leroy thought harder and harder.

Then he shouted out: "It's Ronnie!"

Leroy was right.

Ronnie, a man who lives in the warden-assisted flats called Morningdale Court, is one of their favourite neighbours in The Crescent. He has to use a wheelchair because he has injured his legs. Sometimes he walks with crutches but only for a short distance.

"Now it's my turn," said their daddy. "I'm thinking of two names. They both begin with a letter 'J', and they live at this house."

That was easy for Leroy and Linda to guess because their daddy had given them an important clue.

"Josh, that's you, daddy," they both shouted, "and the other is Jenny, our big sister."

The twins were right again.

"What letter does my name begin with?" asked their mummy. She was carrying a large bowl of strawberries, melons and grapes.

"B, because your name is Brenda," laughed the twins.

Now they were interested in why their mummy had such a huge bowl of fruit. "B is for bowl too," she said.

And then she explained.

"It is nearly the end of the summer holidays. Soon you will be starting school, and I thought it would be nice to have a street party. This fruit is for us all to eat. Paul's grandma, Matti, says she will make a big Crescent cake, just like the shape of our street. She will make little houses and flats out of sugar icing and marzipan to decorate the cake. Dr. Benson has said he will make curried potato cakes, and Mr Allsorts will give us lots of crisps and drinks."

Mr Allsorts is the name the children have given to Mr Alsop, who runs the corner shop, because he sells everything.

"Susie's grandparents will bring lots of surprises, and perhaps balloons," Brenda continued. "And the students have promised to make a very exotic pudding with pineapples and coconut milk."

Sali and Tim will also bring some savoury filo pastries and sesame snaps that they have baked themselves.

"Oo!" said Leroy and Linda, with big smiles.

They were very happy.

"What shall we make?" they asked.

"You can make pin-on badges and write the first letter of everyone's name on them," she said. And she reached into her bag and pulled out a big handful of pin-on badges.

"Be careful with the writing," said their mummy. "Do it in pencil first so that we can rub it out if it's wrong. After that you can use the felt pens to colour in the letters on the badges."

And that is what they did.

The twins worked all day. They made some beautiful letter name badges with patterns on them.

They even made badges for Sophie, the blind woman, who also lives in The Crescent, and for Hope, the dog that guides her. Both badges had writing in bright yellow fluorescent colour.

"Wonderful!" said their daddy when he saw what they had done.

"That is excellent," said Jenny, their big sister. "I will have to write about your hard work in my journal."

The twins liked the idea of Jenny writing about them in her journal. The next day was party day. All the people who lived in The Crescent came, and they all wore the first letter name badges that Linda and Leroy had made. They played a guessing game, and tried to guess each other's names.

But by now YOU already know the names of some of the people who live in The Crescent.

Lesson 2: August

> **Story: The New Beginning**
> **Theme: New beginnings**

Synopsis

The twins, Leroy and Linda, have 'butterflies in their tummies' because it is the first day at school. Others also have new beginnings, but there is no one as new as Shama's kittens who are newly born. This is a story about different kinds of new experiences.

Objectives

- To recognise what pupils like and dislike.

- To share their opinions on things that matter to them.

- To recognise and name their feelings.

- To take part in discussions.

- To understand how rules help them.

- To realise that people and other living things have needs and they have a responsibility to meet them.

- To understand about growing from young to older and to realise that people's needs change.

- To identify the differences between people.

Preparing for the story

The children sit in a circle with adult helpers and the teacher. In some cases a child will pass round the speaking object or mouthpiece while in other cases the teacher can choose a volunteer. This preparation is quite long and it is advised that it should be done as one discrete session or lesson. During the preparation the feelings associated with new experience and some of the sensations involved in that experience are explored.

To show and to see

The teacher shows the children something new and something old in that order. The teacher shows them something to feel, see and hear.

To feel

The teacher introduces the sensation of touch. A feely bag or box may be used. The teacher drops a small item into the bag, for example a lychee or hard kiwi fruit or something rough in texture. The teacher asks the children to feel the object in the bag without looking; the children are asked to close their eyes whilst the bag is passed around. Is this a good experience? Do the children like it? Teachers, helpers and children discuss what it feels like to touch something that one can't see. The teacher may want to liken it to being blind, like Sophie Sellars in The Crescent or the blindness of kittens at birth.

To see

Something new should be introduced: perhaps a new coin, a new pair of shoes or a purchase still in the sealed packet. The teacher tells the children that they have now seen something new. Then the teacher will introduce something old (for example, an antique object or picture). Although this object should be old it should be new to the child in terms of visual experience, i.e. the children have never seen it before and they don't know what it is. The teacher discusses with the children how they have deduced it is an old or new object, i.e. what process they have gone through. Perhaps they found clues. The new object might be clean, unused and shiny, whilst the old object may show signs of use.

To hear

The teacher could find a scarf or fragment of material and place it on his or her knee to hide a small piece of bubble wrap, which creates a popping sound when pressed, and a plastic bottle containing small objects which creates a rattling sound. In turn the children discuss the sounds and guess what is making them.

To tell

Now is the time to tell of new experiences. The children can be asked to think of new experiences, something they have done for the first time in their memory, for example started school, chosen a pet, gone to an unknown place on holiday. Did they like the experience? How do they feel when they experience something new? Is it exciting? Can it be a bit scary?

PSHE
1a, c. 2a.

44

Revise and recap the previous session

'Preparing for the story' may have been dealt with in a previous session. Now is the time to recap and revise the ideas. The teacher could say something like the following:

> "We talked previously about new experiences, about new things and about old things and what it was like to see, feel and hear old and new things. We looked at… Then we talked about new experiences, about our first day at school or in a new class, about going to a café or restaurant for the first time and about new places we have been to on holiday. Some of you spoke about going on a ship, plane or train for the first time. Now I am going to read you a story about the people and animals in The Crescent and about how they experienced some new beginnings."

Read the story

The teacher reads the story to the children.

Circle Time discussion

Question 1 Is it very hard to start at a new school?

Is it hard or easy to meet new people? In what ways is it hard or easy to meet new people? Why are some people more 'scary' than others? How does it feel when you start a new school and you meet someone you know perhaps from playgroup or nursery school? What was a hard part of your first day for you, or an easier part of your first day for you? What did you feel when it was home time?

PSHE
1a, 1c, 2a.

English 1.
1a, b, c. 2a, c, d. 3a, c.

Question 2 Why do we need rules?

Would shouting or running in school be nice for other people? Are there times when we can run or jump (playtime) and times when we might sit quietly? Is it good to have some quiet times? What things can we do at playtime or in PE sessions that would not be good for other children in lesson time or in assembly? Can rules help you?

PSHE
2a, d.

English 1.
1a, b, c. 2a, c, d. 3a, c.

Question 3 Becky was very new because she didn't know anyone. How could she be helped?

Is it good to share with your friends? Do you think Becky felt more alone than the other children did because she had not been to the same nursery school or playgroup and she knew no one else at all? Was it part of the other children's responsibilities to help Becky?

PSHE
2a, c.

English 1.
1a, b, c. 2a, c, d. 3a, c.

Question 4 Is it nice to be made welcome?

PSHE
1a. 1c. 2a.

English 1.
1a, b, c. 2a, c, d.
3a, c.

What makes you feel welcome? Is it good to see welcome signs such as pictures at a new school, or tea and orange squash and cakes or biscuits when you come home from school? Are some signs not welcoming like 'BEWARE OF THE DOG' or 'KEEP OFF THE GRASS' or 'TRESPASSERS WILL BE PROSECUTED?' How do they make you feel?

Question 5 Can you think of some 'welcome' ideas?

If a new person came to live near you could you make or buy a card that said 'Welcome to Your New Home'? Does your school have space for pictures and posters that welcome others? Are some things welcoming and some things not welcoming? Give some examples.

PSHE
1a, c.

Is a smile, or hug or a handshake welcoming? How do people greet each other? How do you like to be greeted?

Is a scowl welcoming? Does it make you feel happy?

Question 6 Do you think that Leroy and Linda's mummy was nervous because she was starting a new job?

PSHE
1a, c.

Can you remember the story? Was Linda and Leroy's mummy nervous? Was it right that Linda and Leroy's mummy should have butterflies in her tummy? Does being an older person make it easier to experience new things? Who do you think was the most nervous and why?

Supplementary ideas

A washing line may be fixed in the classroom. Cards with numbers from 0-10 could be hung up, by an adult, on the washing line.

PSHE
1a, c. 3d.

Maths 2.
2a.

Link each number to a year in a child's life. Discuss what would be a good and wanted present at each age. For instance would a four year old prefer a present of a swing or a calculator? Would a one-year-old child want a GameBoy or some cot blankets? Some presents will be sensible for the age and others will be silly. Ask the children if an appropriate present might make someone happy. Do the children like giving presents? Do the children like receiving presents? Russian dolls can be used to illustrate the concept of bigger and smaller.

Ask the children what baby cats, dogs, and pigs and cows are called. What makes them happy?

A kitten likes milk.

A puppy likes treats and milk.

A calf likes a green field and milk.

A piglet likes mud and milk.

Are they the same, different or both?

What makes the children happy? Do different things make different people and animals happy?

PSHE
4c.

Would a kitten like the same thing as an adult? Does a child like the same things as an adult?

The teacher divides the class into groups in the classroom. One able or older child, teacher or helper will act as reader, leader or scribe. Think of some good rules and some silly rules. For example:

- Never run in the classroom.

- Share with other children.

- Shout at your friends.

- Be kind to new children.

- Call other children nasty names.

All groups come together. The leader of each group shares ideas with the class. Now, with the teacher, the children select some important rules. The teacher writes down and displays the resulting code of conduct in a prominent place in the classroom.

PSHE
2d.

Memories of the children's first day at school can be discussed. How did they feel? Was it difficult to know where rooms were and where equipment was kept? Did certain events result in different emotions like happiness, sadness, or loneliness? How did they feel at the end of the day? Was it good to be going home? What made them feel welcome? Perhaps it was a picture, poster or caption on the wall or something a teacher, adult helper or headteacher said. What new things did the child encounter?

The children can draw a picture of themselves on their first day in school or in a new class. What emotions are they feeling? The teacher asks the children who would like to display their picture to the class and discusses their ideas, feelings and emotions and how they have portrayed them.

Worksheet instructions

"The kittens are discovering new things every day. Today they have found something that they have never seen before. They have found a ball of wool. They have also knocked over a box of crayons and pencils, which have scattered all over the floor. Now they are playing with them. You can see two big squares on the worksheet. In one square draw something that you used to play with when you were younger. Now draw something in the other square that is new to you and that you have just discovered. It might be a new friend, a new toy or a new activity. It can be anything that is new to you. Now colour the picture."

(Volunteer children can display their worksheet to the class and talk about the old and new things in the picture.)

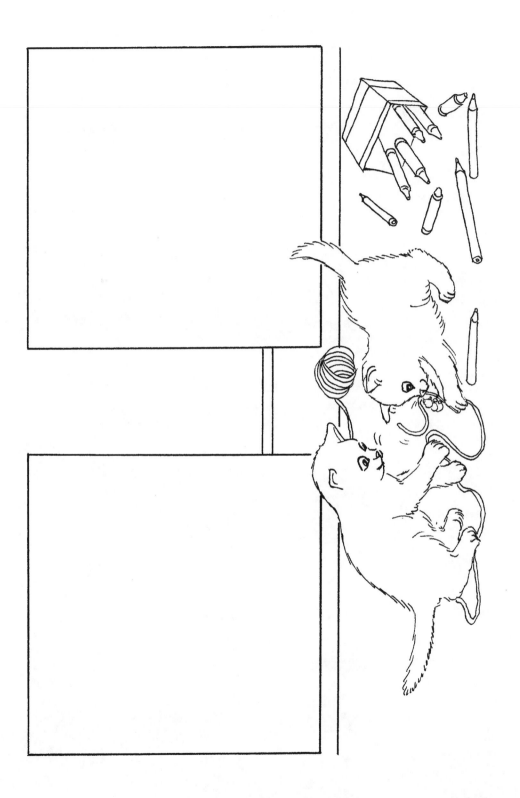

49

The New Beginning

The twins were very excited.

"We are going to start big school tomorrow," said Leroy.

"We are both going to start school tomorrow," echoed Linda.

They jumped up and down shouting.

"We're going to school! We're going to school!" over and over again.

The next day, as their mummy was taking them to school for the very first time, Leroy said, "I feel a bit sick."

"I feel a bit sick, too," moaned Linda.

"I think that you will feel better soon. Everybody feels strange when they are starting something new," their mummy explained.

Then she told Leroy and Linda that their big sister, Jenny, was starting a new class.

"I expect that Jenny is feeling a bit nervous too," she said.

"Yes, but she's not new like we are," protested Linda. "Jenny has been going to Riley Green School for ages."

"That's what I think too," said Leroy. "Jenny is not really new. She is not really, really new."

"You two do look smart in your new school clothes," said Brenda. She was the twins' mummy. She was trying to change the subject.

"But my tummy is very sick," wailed Leroy.

"We should go back home, mummy, because I'm getting more sick as well," Linda complained.

"We can't do that," said Brenda, "because I am going to start my new job today. I am going to be an assistant warden at Morningdale Court. That is something very new for me as well."

Just for a minute the twins stopped complaining and listened to their mummy.

"I've got butterflies in my tummy," she said.

"Well you are old, mummy," said Linda thoughtfully, "so you will be alright."

"Yes, you are old, mummy, not new like us. Your butterflies are not like mine. Anyway I've got big buzzy bees in my tummy," Leroy argued.

Soon they were at the school gates. All the new children were arriving. Leroy and Linda knew some of the children. They had all been to the same playgroup.

"There's Oscar," shouted Leroy looking about. "And Daniel and William are here too."

Linda had seen Emily, her friend from playgroup. Emily was hiding behind her daddy's back.

Mrs Dickinson, the teacher, showed the children where to hang their coats. Leroy and Linda were very surprised, because there, next to their coat peg was a photograph of themselves.

"Hello children!" said Mrs Dickinson when the children were all in the classroom. "You are all new children today, but this is Becky. She is very new because she has only just come to live in Riley Green."

All the children had a busy first day at school. They had so many children's names to try to remember. Even Mrs Dickinson kept making mistakes. She called Linda, 'Lydia,' by mistake. She called Leroy, 'Liam,' by mistake. That made the twins laugh.

When Brenda met the twins from school they looked quite tired, but they were not complaining.

"Our teacher makes mistakes," Leroy laughed.

"When we get back home you can tell me all about your new day," said Brenda, "and I will tell you about my new job."

They had not been at home for more than a few minutes when the doorbell rang.

It was Shama from Number 9 The Crescent.

"Would Linda and Leroy like to see the new kittens?" she asked. "Crocus, my tortoiseshell cat, gave birth to them this morning."

Leroy and Linda ran out of the house without waiting a second. They certainly wanted to see the new kittens.

Shama told the children that there were two new kittens, and that their names were Opus and Rumpus. There was one boy kitten and one girl kitten.

"Twins, like us," shouted Leroy excitedly.

"We must be very gentle and quiet," said Shama. "These kittens are very new and Crocus has never had kittens before. She is a bit nervous."

The twins were very quiet. They peeped into the basket where Crocus was looking after her kittens.

"They are so very new," Shama said again.

"They are more new than we were when we started school today," whispered Linda.

"Yes, and more new than Becky," added Leroy.

"You can't be newer than Opus and Rumpus," said Josh, who had crept into Shama's kitchen. He wanted to see the kittens. Then Jenny arrived. She wanted to see the new kittens.

"The kittens want to stay with their mother until they are older," said Shama. "But after a while they will want to go out to learn new things."

The twins nodded. They agreed with Shama.

"There have been so many new things that have happened today," said Josh, as he tucked the twins up into their beds. Then added, "and so many new beginnings."

Lesson 3: September

> **Story: The Ambulance Man's Daughter**
> **Theme: Assumption and Prejudice**

Synopsis

Becky, a new girl at Riley Green infant school, is excluded from play and mocked because of being different. The story explores the feeling of the rejected and shows how successful inclusion can be managed.

Objectives

- To recognise and name feelings.

- To take part in discussion.

- To understand rules and ways of keeping safe and about people who can help them stay safe.

- To identify and respect the differences between people.

- To know that friends should care for one another.

- To learn that there are different types of bullying.

- To recognise that bullying is wrong and how to get help to deal with bullying.

- To feel positive about themselves and having their achievements recognised.

- To deal with feelings in a positive way.

Preparing for the story

The children, teacher and helpers sit in a circle. The teacher should have something from the first-aid cupboard or box to show to the children, for example a bandage, safety pin, triangular bandage or an eye patch. Discuss with the children what these items are for, that is to say which item should be used for which injury. Demonstrate how the items would be used. Discuss from whom the children would seek help for a physical injury. For example would they ask for help from a parent, a school nurse or a teacher? Think about when and how the emergency services should be called. Would they be called for a cold or a splinter in your hand? What if someone was unconscious or had been hit by a car and couldn't walk? Remind the children of the number to call. After these issues encourage the children to think of other ways that one can feel pain, hurt or discomfort even though there is no physical sign of injury. Can one feel pain if one's feelings are hurt? (In the story Becky feels the pain of exclusion and she knows what to do for a physical injury.)

PSHE
2a. 3g.

Read the story

After the above activity has been completed the teacher reads the story to the children.

Circle Time discussion

Question 1 Who was hurt in the story and who helped Linda? What did Leroy feel?

PSHE
1c. 2a. 3g.

English 1.
1a, b, c. 2a, c, d.
3a, c.

Was Linda hurt in the story and did Becky help her? Did Becky know what to do? Why did Becky know what to do? Was Linda hurt on purpose or was it an accident? Did Leroy feel happy or sad and guilty when Linda was hurt? Who had special knowledge? What did Becky do first? Do you think that Becky felt happy because she could help? Did she know who was the right person to ask for help?

Question 2 Do you think it is nice to be alone all the time or just sometimes?

PSHE
1c. 2a.

English 1.
1a, b, c. 2a, c, d.
3a, c.

Do you always need other people? Are there times when you would rather be alone? Can other people sometimes help you? Can other people make you happy, angry, sad etc.? Do we sometimes want to be alone if we are sad? If we are angry do we sometimes need some time on our own to calm down? What do we like to do when we are alone (read comics, play a game, play with the cars or doll's-house etc?) If you are physically hurt do you need others? What can someone else do to make you happy if you feel sad? Can other people alter your mood? Is it good to share a joke, a smile or a story? Are there times when jokes are not appropriate? Would a joke be the right thing to tell if someone was hurt?

Question 3 If you had to telephone the emergency service which number would you ring and what information would you give?

Here the teacher is looking for factual information. Would you ring 999? Would you say what service was needed: police, ambulance or fire brigade? What service would you need if someone was hurt? Would it be important to tell the operator your name, where you are and what has happened?

PSHE
2a. 3g.

English I.
Ia, b, c. 2a, c, d. 3a, c.

Question 4 Can we be hurt in different ways?

Have you ever been hurt? Are there different ways of being hurt? Have you ever been hurt physically? Have your feelings ever been hurt? Do different things make us better? Can a bandage make us better if we have a sore knee? Can a bandage make us better if someone has called us a name? Can someone make us feel better by being our friend or saying something comforting to us if we are afraid or angry?

PSHE
Ic. 2a.

English I.
Ia, b, c. 2a, c, d. 3a, c.

Question 5 What is first-aid, why is it called this?

Is first-aid meant to help the person who is hurt? Is there any order in which we should do things? Do we make sure the person who is hurt is warm and comfortable? Is there always a person there who can help like a doctor, or a nurse? Should a teacher be sent for if someone is hurt? Are some injuries much worse than others?

PSHE
2a. 3g.

English I.
Ia, b, c. 2a, c, d. 3a, c.

Question 6 Did Mrs Dickinson blame the children who had not been kind to Becky?

Did Mrs Dickinson tell the children that Becky had been sad? Is bullying always wrong? Did she ask the children what might make Becky happy? Do you think the others had some good ideas about how to make Becky happy? If she had been angry with the people who had not been kind to Becky and bullied her would it have been helpful to Becky? How might the other children have felt? Did the story have a happy ending? Do you think Mrs Dickinson had some good ideas to stop others bullying Becky?

PSHE
Ic. 2a. 4e.

English I.
Ia, b, c. 2a, c, d. 3a, c.

Supplementary ideas

Becky was rejected by others; they wouldn't let her play because she was different. In the classroom, discuss how she felt when she was rejected. Discuss with the children about loneliness and ask if they think that excluding is a type of bullying. Now arrange the children into groups for an art lesson. Cut out two circles of card or use paper plates. On one piece of card or paper plate draw Becky when she is sad and lonely and on another piece of card or paper plate draw Becky when she is happy because she is accepted by her new friends. These can be displayed in the classroom, or a stick puppet can be made for each child by placing a stick between the two circular cards or paper plates and using a strong glue to construct your puppet. A model out of clay or plasticine of Becky in the playground could be made by each child. Is Becky happy or sad?

PSHE
1c. 4d.

Becky did not know all her numbers but she knew all her letters. In class, discuss with the children the notion that we all know different things and that everybody's contribution is different. The children work independently for this task as the exercise asks for each individual child to explain what they know. Give the child four sheets marked 'Letters I Know'. 'Numbers I Know', 'Words I Know' and 'Sums I Know'. Encourage the child to express what he or she knows. This might be dated and either entered into the child's record of achievement or into their folder of Crescent worksheets.

PSHE
4c. 5b.

The teacher makes some large worksheets of affirmative comments and unpleasant comments. Some examples are:

'Well done.'
'I think you are smelly.'
'Welcome.'
'Go away I don't like you.'
'You have chosen healthy food.'
'Your ideas are silly.'

In groups of four with someone acting as scribe, the children discuss which are affirmative comments and which ones are caring, and then mark them with a tick. Are affirmative comments kind and friendly? Unpleasant comments are marked with a big red cross. The teacher collects all the worksheets and displays and discusses them with the class.

PSHE
2a, 4d.

The teacher discusses with the class about why and how we keep safe. Some rules for keeping safe could be written. What does 'keep safe' mean? What rules could we make to keep safe? Which people could we go to if we needed to keep safe? Should we avoid some things (like playing 'chicken', crossing busy roads, walking on frozen water and trespassing)? Who might help if you were ill or injured? Should we be alone or in pairs or groups?

PSHE
2a, 3g.

Worksheet instructions

"On the worksheet you will find a first-aid box. Can you see it? It has a large cross on the front of the box. The cross should be coloured red. Look at the little pictures on the worksheet. Which things belong in the box? You will see some 'get well medicine' in a bottle, if you think it belongs in the box draw a line from the 'get well medicine' to the box. Now do the same for the other things."

The Ambulance Man's Daughter

All the children were playing together in the playground except for one little girl, who was all on her own.

No one was playing with Becky. Becky stayed close by her teacher. She held on to Mrs Dickinson's hand. Becky was new to Riley Green. She had just moved with all her family to a house in Weston Park Road. She had had lots of friends at her old house in Sunny Vale. She had been to nursery school there. She had known many other children. They had all been her friends. But here in Riley Green she had no friends and some of the children told Becky to go away.

Sometimes Leroy and Linda, the twins, played with Becky, but today they were playing tag with all the friends they knew well. Becky watched Linda as she ran round and round the playground laughing as Rosie nearly caught her.

Becky made herself very brave. She let go of her teacher's hand. She ran up to Rosie and asked if she could play.

"No you can't," said Rosie unkindly.

"Lots of people are playing now and there isn't room for anyone else," said Rachel, even though that was not true. Only six children were playing and one more could easily have played.

The bell rang and the children lined up. A teacher was there to bring them safely into school.

"I don't want to stand next to Becky," said Rosie, and she pushed in front of Carla instead.

"Becky's fat," said Rachel quietly so the teacher couldn't hear, but Becky could.

Poor Becky. She wasn't at all fat, but she felt terrible. Was she really fat she wondered. She stood up straight and breathed in.

In the cloakroom things got worse for Becky.

"You can't even do your shoelaces," said Rosie. This was true. At her other school Becky had not been taught how to tie shoe laces.

"But I can button up my coat," said Becky bravely.

"You can't even count to ten," said Rachel, who had noticed that Becky had got her numbers all wrong that morning.

"I know all my letters though," said Becky.

"Becky can't do her work," chanted Rosie and Rachel unkindly.

"I can," said Becky, "I can. I can. I can."

Just then Mrs Dickinson came down to the cloakroom to see why all her girls were taking so long.

"It's Becky," said Rosie, giving Becky a threatening look and a quiet nip. "She's feeling sick."

Mrs Dickinson said nothing to Rosie but she smiled at Becky.

"Do you feel well enough to come into the classroom?" asked Mrs Dickinson.

"Yes," said Becky bravely choking back her tears.

In the classroom Becky stayed close to her teachers. Mrs Dickinson noticed that only Linda talked to Becky. Linda knew how mean the others were and it worried her. But to make things worse Rachel became quite nasty to Linda because she could see that Linda was being nice to Becky.

"If you're friends with Becky you can't be friends with us," said Rachel to Linda.

Linda was a bit scared. What if the other children wouldn't play with her? She would hate that. So Linda talked to Becky when she thought no one was looking. She wondered what to do. I know, she thought, I'll find a time when I'm alone with Mrs Dickinson and tell her all about it. She would know what to do. She would tell her teacher how mean the others were to Becky. Linda didn't think it was fair on Becky. After all Becky couldn't help not knowing everything they had been taught at St. Thomas' Playgroup. Linda felt sure that Becky must have learnt things that she didn't know.

All afternoon until playtime Becky stayed close to her teacher. When Mrs Dickinson moved to the cupboard Becky moved there as well.

"Becky's a baby," said Rachel to Linda. "Look how she stayed near to Mrs Dickinson."

Afternoon playtime arrived. Mrs Dickinson rushed out to get her cup of tea from the staff room before she went on duty in the playground. Becky was left alone. She took a long time in the cloakroom putting on her coat. She decided she would stay out of the way of everybody. She would just stand in the doorway and watch the others play. In the playground Linda was playing tag with Carla, Rosie and Rachel. She was wondering how to tell her teacher that Becky was being bullied. Would Mrs Dickinson believe her? Would the others be nasty to her if she was friendly with Becky? Linda was wondering about these things so much that she had forgotten to put her coat on and it was just beginning to rain. She didn't see Leroy, Simon and Bethany running towards her. Leroy and Linda ran straight into each other. Linda fell over. She felt a terrible pain in her knee.

"Oh, my leg. It hurts," she cried.

"It must be broken," shouted Simon.

"Get up and try to walk," yelled Rachel and Rosie in a panic.

"You'll get in trouble now, Leroy," shouted Bethany. "You pushed her over."

"Oh, look there's blood coming out of your knee," cried Carla as Leroy tried to pull Linda to her feet.

Then, quietly but firmly, Becky's voice could be heard. Becky knew exactly what had to be done because her Dad was an ambulance driver and he had taught her first-aid.

"Linda, just sit down and be quiet until we fetch a teacher," said Becky. "Rosie, go and tell Mrs Dickinson what has happened. I don't think your leg is broken," said Becky soothingly to Linda. "Leroy, lend Linda your coat to keep her warm."

Leroy took his coat off right away and put it round Linda's shoulder. He was glad he could do something to help. He looked very pale. He hadn't meant to hurt Linda. Neither of them had been looking where they were going.

Suddenly Mrs Dickinson was there. She looked at and felt Linda's leg. "It's alright," she said. "Linda's leg's not broken. It's just badly grazed. We'll soon make it better. Help me walk Linda into school, Becky," she said.

In school Mrs Dickinson unlocked the first-aid box. She washed Linda's knee and put some lint on it. She bandaged it nicely. Linda stopped crying and told her teacher how she hadn't been looking where she was going because she was thinking how nasty the others were to Becky.

"Don't say anything to them," pleaded poor Becky. "It'll make things worse for me."

"I will not say anything which will make things bad for you and Linda," promised Mrs Dickinson, as they walked to the classroom.

In the classroom Rosie, Rachel and Carla were playing in the home corner. Mrs Turner, the nursery nurse was there.

"Can Linda and Becky play with us?" they asked.

They all played together. Linda sat down on a red chair and Rachel and Becky made her a pretend cup of tea, with lots of sugar in it. Rosie and Carla put the dolls to bed and wrapped a bandage round teddy's leg because he had fallen on the pavement. Later on they all played with the construction toys. Rosie and Becky made a house together. It had red doors and blue windows. They put some people inside and some children playing outside.

"See," said Rosie. "They are all playing together."

Just before home time Mrs Dickinson spoke to Carla, Rosie and Rachel. She told them that Becky had been sad and asked if they could think of any ways to make her happy again.

The girls thought of many good ideas.

"I'll let Becky play with us all the time," said Rosie.

"I'll teach her how to do shoelaces," said Rachel.

"She can share my crisps," said Carla. "After all, it must be hard being new and she saved Linda's life."

Lesson 4: September

Story: The 'Not About Us' Story
Theme: Territory and Trespass

Synopsis

Linda and Leroy can't be pleased so Ronnie, a disabled neighbour, tells them a story. The story is about children who won't share their territory with one another. After a restorative sleep, during which time 'Happy Flower Seeds' are planted, the pair learn to share and to laugh at themselves. They finally disclaim their negative feelings by saying the story is 'not about us'. The story is about the needs for defensible space, and yet the positive nature of sharing it with friends.

Objectives

- To recognise what they like and dislike and what is fair and unfair.

- To share their opinions on things that matter to them and explain their views.

- To take part in discussion.

- To make simple choices that improve their health and wellbeing.

- To understand that family and friends should care for one another.

- To feel positive about themselves and enjoy the relaxation they gain.

Preparing for the story

This exercise will take place in the hall. Some of the space will be taken by a circle of chairs - one for each child and helper. The children find themselves a space in the hall. This space will be their own space. The children lie on the floor in their own space and close their eyes; they will feel their bodies, relax and breathe deeply. The teacher tells the children that they have to pretend that they have had a lovely day but now they feel tired. The teacher can say the following words:

> "Imagine that the day is warm and sunny. You are lying on a sun bed or blanket in a beautiful garden. Imagine the type of flowers which are planted there. What colour are your flowers? Imagine the smell or fragrance of the flowers. The flowers have just the right amount of water, light and good food to make them big and strong and healthy. What is the stem like? Is it straight and strong? Do the roots spread into the ground to get their food and water? Imagine how the leaves look, are they a light green, a yellowish green or a dark green? Imagine your flowers, what is the shape like, how are the petals formed and what colour are they? Are they moving in the breeze, or are they very still and quiet? For a few minutes relax and imagine the flowers that are growing in your garden. You are a nice person and your flowers are nice."

(After two minutes have passed, or a period of the teacher's choice, the teacher says the following):

> "You will have thought about and pictured your beautiful flowers. In your own time wake up slowly and sit up. Think about how you felt when you were relaxing. One by one over the next few minutes, and without saying a word, find a seat in the circle. Sit comfortably and think of your flowers and how you felt."

(The teacher can adjust the script to fulfil the needs of the children in his care.) When all children are quiet the mascot is passed around the circle and only when they are holding the mascot, (which may be a talking bird) can each participant speak. The teacher will start first and he will tell everyone about his flowers. The teacher, and later the children, will tell everyone how they felt when they were relaxed. Did they like the feeling? Do they sometimes like to be on their own? Are there other times when they enjoy people's company? The children should each have a turn to speak, but can 'pass' if they want to.

PSHE
la. 2a. 5b.

Read the story

After the above activity has been completed the teacher reads the story to the children.

Circle Time discussion

Question 1 Do you like stories?

Do you like stories being read to you, and/or stories that you read? Do you like it when someone tells you a story from their own memory and does not use a book?

PSHE
la, b. 2a.

English I.
la, b, c. 2a, c, d.
3a, c.

Question 2 What sort of stories do you like?

Do you like scary or nice gentle stories? Do you like realistic stories or fairy tales?

PSHE
la, b. 2a.

English I.
la, b, c. 2a, c, d.
3a, c.

Question 3 Do you think that Linda and Leroy were too tired to share at the beginning of the story?

Is it hard to share if you are tired? Are there other times when it's hard to share? Can you remember a time when you couldn't share?

PSHE
Ib. 2a.

English I.
la, b, c. 2a, c, d.
3a, c.

Question 4 Do we all need plenty of time to sleep?

Do we all need the same amount of sleep? Does a good sleep make us feel well and healthy? Should we all make sure that we have sufficient sleep time? Should we go to bed when our mum or dad tells us it is time to go to bed?

PSHE
2a, 3a.

English I.
la, b, c. 2a, c, d.
3a, c.

Question 5 Why did Leroy and Linda laugh?

Were Leroy and Linda laughing at themselves a bit? Do you think they thought that they could share? Is it fair to share? Do you share? Did they not like to think that the story was about them?

PSHE
la, 2a.

English I.
la, b, c. 2a, c, d.
3a, c.

Supplementary ideas

The following exercise can take place in the classroom with children being gathered round the teacher, possibly on the carpet. The teacher has two lists, which he shows to the children. One is headed 'Times when it is best to be alone' and the other is headed 'Times when it is best to be with other people'. The teacher asks for contributions from the children about being alone and being with other people. It may be best to be alone if they are tired, cross or angry or if they need to rest. It may be best to be with other people when they need to share, play games, take turns, talk or tell secrets. Do other people sometimes need to be on their own or with others? Should we try to include others when they want to be part of a group? The teacher acts as scribe and when the two lists are complete they can be displayed on the classroom wall.

PSHE
1b. 2a, e. 4d.

English 1.
1b. 2a, c, d.
3a, c.

The children sit on the carpet and the teacher explains that they are going to think about characters in fairy stories. Were they able to share? For example was Goldilocks able to share or the Three Bears, or Cinderella, or The Ugly Sisters or the wolf in the story of Red Riding Hood? Were their characters fair or unfair? Is it fair or unfair to share? The teacher might want to have a large sheet on which the characters from fairy tales, that he wants to talk about, are drawn. He can put a tick or a cross against the character if they could share or not share.

PSHE
1a. 2a.

Worksheet instructions

"Some of the people in this worksheet are not next to the tree that is shaped like their head. Some of them are quite cheeky and they are on someone else's territory. Can you see a circle headed person on the square shaped tree, or the square headed person on the triangular shaped tree? Your job is to join the square headed people to the square tree, the circle headed people to the circular tree and the triangular headed people to the triangular tree. This is their territory and they can only go onto someone else's territory if they are invited. When everyone is joined up correctly you can colour the picture."

The 'Not About Us' Story

Linda and Leroy were squabbling. Nothing was pleasing them.

Their mother couldn't please them.

Josh couldn't please them.

Jenny couldn't please them.

Ronnie, who had been invited for tea, said that he would try to please them.

He had brought his large drawing book and his special marker pens.

"I think I will write you a picture story," he said. And so he began.

Once upon a time there were some twins. They looked rather miserable.

There was Linda Longface.

And there was Leroy Longface.

Nothing would please them and they did not like each other.

So Linda Longface went this way.

And Leroy Longface went that way.

Linda Longface said: "I'm going to this part of the meadow."

Leroy Longface said: "I'm going to that part of the meadow."

Linda Longface said: "You can't come past my fence."

And Leroy Longface said: "You can't come past my fence."

After a while Linda Longface fell fast asleep.

So Leroy Longface fell fast asleep too.

They went to sleep for a long time because they were very tired Longfaces.

Whilst they were asleep Ronnie Roundsmiley said, "I am going to give Linda Longface a happy laugh. Then she will be called 'Linda Happy Laugh'."

Then he said: "I am going to give Leroy Longface a happy laugh and then he will be called 'Leroy Happy Laugh'."

"Whilst Linda Longface is asleep I will plant some Happy Flower Seeds near her fence."

"Whilst Leroy Longface is asleep I will plant some Happy Flower Seeds near his fence."

And he did.

"Linda Longface will wake up and Leroy Longface will wake up and this is what they will see."

Just then Linda and Leroy, who had been listening and watching Ronnie write the story, did laugh.

"You are both laughing," said Josh.

"You are both laughing," said mum.

"You are both laughing," said Jenny.

"We know," laughed the twins. "Ronnie Roundsmiley made us laugh. He told us a funny story but it wasn't about us though."

Lesson 5: October

> **Story: The Paper Crown**
> **Theme: Vandalism**

Synopsis

The story features the twins Leroy and Linda and the feelings and emotions of the vandal and the vandalised. How can recompense be made? It happens successfully in the story featuring the recreation work of Leroy and his friends.

Objectives

- To recognise what is fair and unfair and what is right and wrong.

- To recognise name and deal with their feelings in a positive way.

- To think about themselves and learn from their experiences.

- To take part in discussion with one other person and the whole class.

- To understand how rules help them.

Preparing for the story

All children sit in a circle. The teacher prepares and gives the each child a picture of a face which is sad, angry or happy. Each child will have the opportunity to tell the group a time when they were sad, happy or angry depending on which picture they are holding.

PSHE
1c. 2a.

English 1.
1a, b, c. 2a.

Read the story

After the above activity has been completed the teacher reads the story to the children.

Circle Time discussion

PSHE
1a, c. 2a. 4a. 5g.

English 1.
1a, b, c. 2a, c, d.
3a, b, c.

Question 1 How do you think Linda felt when her crown was destroyed?

Did Linda feel sad or happy? Was it fair of Leroy to destroy Linda's crown? Have you ever done something which made another person sad or happy?

PSHE
1a, c. 2e. 4a.

English 1.
1a, b, c. 2a, c, d.
3a, b, c.

Question 2 How do you think Linda felt when Leroy made her another crown?

Do you think Linda felt it was fair that Leroy should make her another crown? Was it right that Leroy should make Linda another crown? How do you think Leroy would feel when he made Linda another crown?

PSHE
1a, b. 2a, c. 4a, d.

English 1.
1a, b, c. 2a, c, d.
3a, b, c.

Question 3 Is it good to forgive?

Did Linda forgive Leroy? How do you know she forgave Leroy? (She helped him to make another crown). Have you ever forgiven someone? Does it feel good to forgive?

PSHE
2a, f. 4d.

English 1.
1a, b, c. 2a, c, d.
3a, c.

Question 4 Who helped Leroy to make the crown?

Could he make the crown all alone or did he need help? Did relatives, friends and neighbours help Leroy? Is it good to have friends? Is it good to belong to groups and communities?

PSHE
2a. 3e.

English 1.
1a, b, c. 2a, c, d.
3a, c.

Question 5 Do you know the names of parts of the body?

The crown is another name for the head (Jack fell down and broke his crown). Head is the name of a part of the body. Are arm, leg, etc. names of other parts of the body?

Question 6 The class are making a pageant for the whole school to watch. Is this a good idea?

Is it good to make something for other people to watch? Why? Is it good to do something for the whole school? Have you ever done a play or something that other people can watch? Did Leroy and Linda's class make other people happy? Was it nice to include Sophie Sellers and her guide dog? Leroy was a good actor and speaker. What are you good at?

PSHE
1c, d. 2a, f, h.

English 1.
1a, b, c. 2a, c, d. 3a, c.

Supplementary ideas

Leroy made Linda a new crown. The teacher arranges the children into pairs. Each child will design and make a crown for the other child. The teacher will provide card, scissors, glue, collage materials, coloured paper etc.

PSHE
4b, d. 5f.

Art & Design
2c. 5a.

The teacher sits at the front of the class. She draws a picture of the human body on paper or the blackboard, asks the children the names of parts of the human body and labels them.

PSHE
3e.

Leroy and Linda have to obey the following rules in their class:

- Never run in the classroom.

- Work hard and consider others.

- Be kind to other people.

- Look after school property and other people's things.

The teacher writes out these rules on the blackboard, whiteboard or a large sheet of paper, and displays the rules at the front of the class. She reads the rules to the children pointing to each word as it is said. The children must put their hand in the air if they think that the rule was broken by Leroy in the story.

Worksheet instructions

"On the worksheet you will find a drawing of a stage. Draw some of the characters who took part in the pageant on the stage. You may want to draw Leroy as a town crier or Linda as the queen. Is Sophie Sellars there with her guide dog Hope? Underneath the picture of the stage is a picture of Linda with her crown. Complete and colour the pictures."

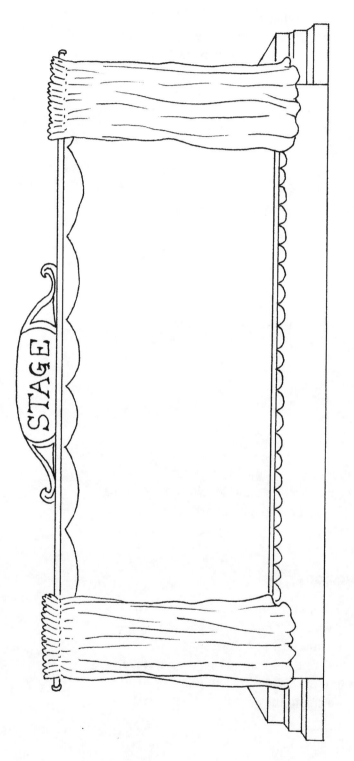

The Paper Crown

Mrs Dickinson looked up from what she was doing. She was astounded. She couldn't see Leroy anywhere in the classroom. She knew that he had been sitting in his place a few minutes earlier.

"Where is Leroy?" she asked her class.

It was nearly home time. They had all been rehearsing for a school pageant called 'Yesterday and Today'.

The children did not know where Leroy was. Neither did Linda, his twin sister. She started to worry, and wondered if Leroy was alright.

Leroy was not alright. He was furious. He was hiding behind a cupboard in the corner of the classroom, and he was tearing up the paper crown that Linda had made that day.

It had taken her a long time to make and colour and decorate it. She was very proud of her Queen's crown. Mrs Dickinson had chosen Linda to be a queen in the class pageant. She had chosen Leroy's best friend to be a king.

She had given all the children in her class a part in the parade, but because Leroy was a good speaker and actor he had been chosen to be the Town Crier and announce the arrival of the kings and queens, the dukes and duchesses, the mayor and mayoress and all the people in the parade. It was a play about the olden times and of how people dressed differently from how they dress today.

Leroy wanted to be a king, and that is why he was very angry and why he was tearing up Linda's crown.

He was trying to tear the paper very quietly, but it was a bit dusty behind the cupboard.

Tearing the paper disturbed the dust.

"Atishoo! Atishoo!" Leroy sneezed.

All the children looked up. They were surprised to hear a sneeze coming from the corner of their classroom.

Linda was the first to dash to the corner.

"It's Leroy!" she shouted as she ran. "I recognise his sneeze. He must be stuck behind the cupboard. I have got to help him get out."

Mrs Dickinson followed, as did most of the other children. They soon discovered what Leroy was doing.

Oh dear! What a big fuss there was after that and what a commotion!

"Get out at once, Leroy," scolded Mrs Dickinson, and asked him what he thought he was doing.

Linda shouted at Leroy as she tried to pick up the pieces of her paper crown.

"You are a horrid, horrid brother," she yelled.

Leroy looked very dusty and very red faced with embarrassment.

Linda grew very red-faced with anger.

Mrs Dickinson tried her best to settle the class down. She was glad it was almost home time, but she knew she had a problem she would have to try to sort out the next day.

She didn't know what to do. Perhaps she should make Linda a new crown.

"We will all have to think hard about this destruction," said Ronnie to Mrs Dickinson when she explained what had happened.

Ronnie had come to school to meet Leroy and Linda because their mummy and daddy were both busy that day. He had agreed to look after them. Ronnie was good at helping people and he could usually sort out problems. But today he was puzzled.

He also had to get back to Morningdale Court where he lived. Sophie Sellars, the blind lady, who also lived in Morningdale Court, had broken her leg and couldn't take Hope, her guide dog, for a walk.

Ronnie was helping by taking Hope out for her walk every day. He had been doing this for almost six weeks.

Linda and Leroy were going to go with him on the walk that day. Ronnie had prepared sandwiches and bought some milk. He had left them in Sophie's room. They were on Sophie's table ready for Linda and Leroy to eat and drink before their walk.

"Oh! What a big problem we have today," said Ronnie as they all entered Sophie's room. They were a bit late because Mrs Dickinson had talked to Ronnie after school.

Ronnie told Sophie what had happened. Hope wagged her tail. She was really ready for her walk. But no one else was ready.

They still hadn't set off when Josh arrived to collect Leroy and Linda half an hour later.

He was whistling and very happy as usual.

"Had a good walk?" asked their dad. "And a lovely tea as well," he remarked as he noticed the sandwiches on the table.

"I am afraid the twins couldn't eat today," said Ronnie, and we haven't been for our walk either. He then had to tell Josh the whole story.

"I think Leroy tore Linda's crown because he wanted to be a king," said Sophie.

Josh scratched his head.

He wondered what he should do.

Ronnie closed his eyes. He wondered what to do.

Sophie put her head in her hands. She wondered what to do.

Hope stayed quietly at Ronnie's feet. She wondered why he was not taking her out for a walk. She wondered what to do.

Linda and Leroy were not speaking to each other. They didn't know what to do.

"Well, this is Leroy's problem," said Josh at last. "He will have to work it out."

"I can't make paper crowns all by myself," wailed Leroy. "I need some help."

"Well, I will help you," Linda muttered. She still felt hurt, but didn't like to see her brother upset.

"And I will find some nice gold card," said Ronnie, and went off to his room to get some straightaway.

"I will let the children work at my table," said Sophie. "They can make a crown for Linda here in my room."

"And I will take Hope for her walk," said Josh.

Josh was gone for quite some time. When he returned Linda's new crown was almost finished. Ronnie had found some glitter and sequins which made the crown sparkle brightly.

The sandwiches were almost finished too.

"Hey! How about a sandwich for me?" asked Josh as he gobbled the last one on the plate. He was hungry after his walk with Hope.

"Don't worry, Josh," laughed Ronnie. "I've ordered us all a big pizza. It will be here in a few minutes."

"A feast fit for a king," joked Sophie when the pizza arrived.

She was pleased that such good things were happening in her home.

The next week it was time for the school pageant. The children's parents were there, and so was Ronnie, who had been invited.

When the parade began Linda looked very regal dressed in queen's clothes and wearing her golden crown. All the children in the class looked wonderful, but perhaps the best character of all and the one who had the most important part was Leroy, the Town Crier.

"Oyez! Oyez! Oyez! Our pageant is today," he began.

Then he had to announce the arrival of all the people in the parade.

He did it very well and spoke very clearly. Then he paused.

Everyone wondered why. Had he forgotten his words?

But Mrs Dickinson was smiling. She and Leroy had a secret. She nodded to Leroy. The curtain on the stage moved a little. Then in an even louder Town Crier's voice Leroy called out. "Now please welcome our special guests. Walking without her plaster for the first time for six weeks, here is Sophie Sellars. And of course, Hope, her wonderful dog."

Then all the children sang the 'Yesterday and Today' pageant song.

The Pageant Song

Yesterday they wore clothes like these
With pinafores
Down to their knees.
Boys wore breeches,
funny name
Men plus four trousers
For a golfing game
Ladies trimmed tremendous hats
with veils to hide their faces.
Once kings wore wigs.
Then later on
men bought elastic braces.
Today we have our modern clothes.
Some wear dungarees.
Tracksuits are such comfy things
for exercise and ease.
We like the clothes we wear today
So colourful and bright
But now we've dressed up for this pageant play
We hope you like the sight.

Lesson 6: October

> **Story:** The Mallard
> **Theme:** Countryside

Synopsis

In response to the injury of a mallard, Leroy , Linda and Jenny show responsible behaviour by caring for the bird and seeking appropriate help. They gain further information about how to look after wildlife from a reliable source. The story also looks at irresponsible behaviour in the countryside and its consequences.

Objectives

- To investigate what improves and harms the countryside environment and about the ways people can look after the countryside environment.

- To realise that other people and other living things have needs and that they have responsibilities to meet them.

- To show how responsibilities increase as people get older.

- To investigate rules for keeping safe in the countryside and how responsible people can help them.

Preparing for the story

All children and adult helpers sit in a circle. The teacher has various items placed in a bag. The teacher explains to the children that she has some things in her bag which are 'good' for the countryside, and other things which are 'bad' for the countryside and may pose a danger. The teacher has two large sheets of paper in front of her marked 'good' and 'bad'. She draws each individual item out of the bag and the children must decide if it is 'good' or 'bad' for the countryside. When a child has responded correctly the teacher puts that article on the appropriate sheet. (At a later time the teacher may wish to make a collage or display of items that are 'good' for the countryside or 'bad' for the countryside.)

Some examples of 'good' and 'bad' articles are:

PSHE
2g.

English I.
2a, c, d.

'Good': A blade of grass, leaves, nuts and berries (not poisonous), a sign saying 'Please shut the gate', real flowers or pictures of flowers, pictures of animals, a dog's lead, collar and tag.

'Bad': An old crisp bag, pieces of wire, a plastic bottle, empty cans, an empty matchbox, an old shoe or trainer and litter of any kind.

Read the story

After the above activity has been completed the teacher reads the story to the children.

PSHE
2a, c.

English I.
1a, b, c. 2a, c, d.
3a, b, c.

Circle Time discussion

Question 1 What do you think that animals and birds need?

Do animals and birds need food and water? Do they need shelter and warmth? Do they need love and nurture? Are their needs and wants exactly the same as the children's or are they different?

Question 2 What things were right and wrong in the story?

PSHE
1a, b. 2a, c, e, g.

English I.
1a, b, c. 2a, c, d.
3a, b, c.

Was it right to throw wire into the pond? Was it right to give bird mix to the mallard ducks on the pond? Was it right to find an appropriate person or persons to help care for the injured bird? Was it right for someone to eat a picnic and leave litter? Was it right or wrong for the children to gather the litter and take it away?

Question 3 Are there things which people should remember and rules to keep to when you are in the countryside? What are they?

PSHE
1a. 2a, c, e. 3a.

English I.
1a, b, c. 2a, c, d.
3a, b, c.

Is it right to keep dogs under control? Should you keep to the public footpath across farmland? Is it wrong to light fires? Why? Should you leave animals and machinery alone? Would it be safe to touch some animals or farm machinery? Should you keep quiet in the countryside or play noisy games? Should you keep water clean and free from litter or waste material? (These things can be written, drawn and displayed and make up the basis for the country code.)

PSHE
2a, e. 3g.

English I.
1a, b, c. 2a, c, d.
3a, b, c.

Question 4 Why did Jenny say it wasn't a good idea to put Muriel in Paul's truck?

Would it be a good idea to move an injured animal or person? Would it be a good idea to find appropriate help?

Question 5 What is the RSPB? Are they a responsible organisation?

Does the RSPB look after birds? Are they a 'good' or 'bad' organisation? Do they want fairness or unfairness for birds?

Question 6 Leroy and Linda were responsible. What sorts of responsibilities do you have?

Do the children feed and care for pets at school or home? Do they keep their toys tidy? Does this help their family? Do they pack away after they have been playing or working? Do responsibilities change when the child is older? Do older brothers and sisters have more responsibilities?

Supplementary ideas

The teacher shows the children some toy models or pictures of farm machinery. They discuss each piece of machinery and its possible dangers and its potential for displaying sharp and dangerous parts, or injuring children in any way. The need to stay safe should be emphasised and discussed.

Storybooks which link to a countryside or environmental theme and which provoke discussion and listening skills include the following:

> *Another Fine Mess* by Tony Bonning and published by David & Charles Children's Books.

> *The Snow Lambs* by Debi Gliori published by Scholastic Children's Books.

> *Dinosaurs and all that Rubbish* by Michael Foreman published by Puffin Books.

> *Custer. The true story of a horse* by Deborah King and published by Red Fox.

All these can be read to the children by the teacher.

The following question can be discussed with the children:

Does everybody live in the country or do some people live in towns or cities? The teacher reads the traditional tale Town Mouse and Country Mouse, shows pictures of the town and the country and ask the children where they live. The teacher discusses 'What would it be like to live in the country?' with children who live in towns and

PSHE
1a, 2a, e.

English 1.
1a, b, c. 2a, c, d. 3a, b, c.

PSHE
1a, d. 2a, e, f. 3d.

English 1.
1a, b, c. 2a, c, d. 3a, b, c.

PSHE
2a. 3g.

English 1.
1a, b, c. 2a, c, d. 3a, b, c.

English 2.
6a, b.

PSHE
2a. 4c.

English 1.
1a, d. 3a.

English 2.
6a, b.

Geography
1a, c.

cities, and 'What would it be like to live in the town and city?' with children who live in the country. Children later are asked to paint or draw a picture of the house where they live.

Memory Game

The teacher starts by saying:

> "When I go to the countryside I take care not to drop crisp packets."

Each child in turn then repeats the list of previous items and adds another.

Eight children are organised into groups of four to arrange an art lesson. Some children have access to paint and brushes. These children choose a cow or a horse to paint. One table will contain collage material for the children to use. They choose to make a sheep, a cat, a dog or a bird. Included in the collage material should be furry fabric, tissue paper and cotton wool balls. The rest of the class could do rubbings for house, fences and gates and could also draw and colour their own individual countryside picture. The children will rotate between the groups. The end result of the children's art work is constructed into a collage by the teacher and/or adult helpers. Appropriate captions should be added, for example 'Close the gate'; 'Keep dogs on leads'; 'Look after the animals'; 'Never play with matches or fire'; 'Take your litter home'. The teacher talks to the children about the usefulness of captions, reads what the captions say and shows the children other captions in books, comics and newspapers.

Worksheet instructions

> "Look at your worksheet. In the worksheet are some things which would be harmful to the countryside. Can you see in the picture there is a gate left open so the animals could escape? Can you see some spilt paint which animals could drink? Is there some litter in the picture? Could animals eat the litter or injure themselves on some of the litter? Can you see a fire which is alight? Would that be dangerous? Why? What is that dog doing there? Has it got a collar, name tag or a lead? Should the dog have these things? Could the dog chase other animals? Would that be the dog's fault or the owner's fault? Now I want you to put a circle around all the things that are harmful to the countryside and against the country code."

PSHE
2g.

English 1.
1a. 2a. 3a, b.

PSHE
2e, g.

Art & Design
2a. 4a.

English 2.
1f. 2a.

The Mallard

Leroy and Linda loved visiting the duck pond near the recreation ground. Today they had gone with their stepsister Jenny, who was much older. Paul, who lived next door to them, was there too.

As usual he had brought his truck.

Leroy and Linda had taken some bird mix to feed the ducks and drakes.

A brown duck swam towards them for some food.

"What kind of duck is that?" Linda asked Jenny.

"That's a mallard," said Jenny, who knew about these things.

"Well, what's that then?" asked Leroy, pointing to a very colourful bird swimming close by.

"That's a mallard too," said Jenny.

"How can that be? How can they both be mallards when they are different colours?" asked Paul. "Well, the colourful one is a male mallard, which we call a drake. The brown one is a female mallard. We call her a duck," explained Jenny. "The female mallard is a dull brown so that people and other animals can't see her very well when she's sitting on the nest. That's the way she stays safe."

"That's clever," said Leroy. "Aren't swans clever?"

"They're ducks and drakes not swans," said Jenny with a laugh.

Leroy was always getting things a bit wrong.

"I like swans," said Leroy, taking no notice of Jenny and getting on with feeding the ducks. One duck came very close and splashed the water with its wings. Linda laughed.

It was lovely down by the duck pond. The day was sunny but cold and the children ran around the water's edge. At the far end of the duck pond was a pile of litter. Someone had eaten a picnic and left all their tin foil, crisp packets and drink cans by the water's edge.

"Let's put all this rubbish into Paul's truck and take it to the bin," said Jenny. "It's wrong to throw rubbish into the pond."

They were clearing a second load of rubbish when Leroy nearly stepped on something lying in the long grass. He bent down to look at it more closely.

"It's a swan," said Leroy. "Look at this swan."

"It isn't a swan. It's a female mallard," said Jenny, "because it's brown all over."

The poor creature flapped a little and tried to move towards the pond. But it couldn't use its leg or wing properly.

"Look there's tangled wire in the rushes," said Paul. "I think it must have hurt itself with the wire."

"Somebody must have thrown the wire into the rushes," said Jenny. "And now the poor duck is hurt, look, its wing is cut, and so is its webbed foot."

"Well, we can't leave it here all alone," said Paul. "Let's take it back home in my truck."

But Jenny thought that Paul's truck would be too bumpy, and she didn't know whether the duck should be moved.

Next door to Jenny lived Shama, who was training to be a vet.

"We will go and ask Shama what to do," said Jenny. "She is sure to know."

The four children were quite out of breath when they arrived at Shama's door.

"What's wrong?" asked Shama, who could see they were worried.

"It's a sick swan," said Leroy. "It's lying near the pond. It can't move. Come on, Shama. Come now."

"It's a female mallard, I think," said Jenny importantly.

Shama went with the children, taking a large cardboard box with her.

"This is in case we have to move the duck," she said.

Down at the pond Shama examined the mallard carefully. "I think we should tell the RSPB," she said. "That is the Royal Society for the Protection of Birds. I know the local man. His name is Phil."

"Let's call the duck Muriel," said Paul. "Muriel's a good name for a duck."

So they did.

Shama collected the wire and put it in the bin. She picked up Muriel carefully and put her in the box.

She carried the injured duck home gently.

Phil came round to collect the duck, and said that when it was well again he would take it back to the pond where it had been found.

The children were rather sad to see Phil take Muriel away in the van.

A month later they heard from Phil. He said that Muriel had recovered completely, and that he was ready to take her back to the pond. The children all went to watch. Phil lifted her out of the crate, and put her on the ground. She seemed rather nervous at first, but suddenly she took to the air, flew across to the other side of the pond, and landed next to a male duck. He seemed very pleased to see Muriel.

The children watched the ducks for a while, as they swam around the pond together.

The Phil gave them lots of leaflets about the RSPB. On one leaflet it said in large writing: 'Look after the birds'.

"We will," said the children. "Just like we looked after Muriel."

Lesson 7: November

> **Story:** The Teddy Bears' Picnic
> **Theme:** Giving and Taking

Synopsis

This story features a teddy bear as a transitional object and a medium for expression. It investigates the need to give to those in hospital and the ability of children to share their goods.

Objectives

- To recognise what they like and dislike, what is fair and unfair and what is right and wrong.

- To recognise, name and deal with feelings in a positive way.

- To take part in discussion.

- To recognise choices they can make and what is right and wrong.

- To learn that they belong to various groups and communities.

- To know that family and friends should care for one another.

- To develop relationships through work and play.

Preparing for the story

The teacher brings into class some fairy cakes with soft icing on the top. The teacher tells the children that these cakes are 'special treasure cakes'. Each child is given some cake decorations and a cake with his name written on the cake cup. The teacher tells the children that they are to decorate the cake with sugar strands, sugar stars and jelly diamonds which have been provided for them. The teacher must emphasise that it is a 'special treasure cake'. The finished cakes are then put on a tray. Another adult helper (nursery nurse or teaching assistant) comes in and takes the cakes saying "Aren't these nice?" The children sit round in a large circle. In turn they say how they made their cake, what decorations they used and how they felt when their cake was taken. The adult helper comes in with the cakes and says she had not taken them but only borrowed them to make into a beautiful display. The children are given their 'special treasure cake' at home time.

Read the story

After the above activity has been completed the teacher reads the story to the children.

Circle Time discussion

Question I How were Leroy and Linda feeling at the start of the story?

Were they sad and angry? Were they sad because something was wrong with them or were they sad for other people?

Question 2 Linda told her teddy how she was feeling. Have you got a special friend?

Some people might tell their mum or dad how they are feeling or a brother or sister or a special toy. Have you someone special to tell when you are feeling sad? Is it always the same person or toy?

Question 3 What makes you feel sad? Is it good to say what it is that you are sad about?

Do you feel a lot better if you tell someone why you are feeling sad?

Question 4 Did the children have a happy day at the hospital? What made them happy?

Did they feel happy because they shared the cakes? Is it good to give to people in hospital? What makes you happy?

Question 5 Have you ever needed to go to the doctor or the hospital?

Have you ever been ill or injured? Tell everyone about it. Who helped you?

Question 6 Is it good to share?

What did Leroy and Linda share? Can you think of things that you share?

PSHE
2a. 4a.

English I.
Ia, c. 2a, c, d.
3a, c.

Supplementary ideas

The children sit on the carpet. They recap their experiences at the doctor's surgery or hospital. The children then sit in their places. Each child is given a sheet of paper. The teacher tells the children to imagine that their bear or other special toy has to go to hospital. The task is to design on paper a meal to make their teddy bear feel better and happier. The children are put in groups of four ready for an art lesson. They are given four paper plates and modelling equipment and playdough of different colours. Each group must share the equipment and the playdough fairly so that everyone can make a model meal for their special toy.

PSHE
5f.

Art & Design
2c.

The children sit on the carpet. The teacher tells the children that they are going to imagine they are buying a present for someone in hospital. What would they buy for:

a baby who had just been born?
a little boy who had broken his arm?
an old man or woman who was recovering from an operation?

The suggestions are discussed and the teacher asks why the present would make the person happy.

PSHE
2a. 3d. 4c.

English I.
Ia. 2a, d. 3a.

The children sit on the carpet. They discuss with the teacher the appropriate ways to behave in hospital. The teacher should ask the children questions, for example:

● Should the children run or shout in hospital?

● Is it nice to bring cards and presents?

● Would it be a good idea to play with your car on the floor?

PSHE
Ia. 2a, c. 3g.

The teacher invites the school nurse or other health professional to talk with the children on a subject pertaining to hospitals and illness, especially what the children can do to make other people feel better.

PSHE
5e.

English I.
9a, b.

The children bring their teddy or other soft toy to school. They draw a picture of their favourite soft toy. They complete the sentence either orally or in writing:

I like _____ because _____ .

Worksheet instructions

"The teddy bears have all brought something for the picnic. They have all brought something to share with the other teddy bears. What to you think that they have brought? You will all have your own ideas. They might have brought sandwiches, cakes or drinks. They might have brought biscuits or fruit. Underneath the pictures of the teddy bears you will find a drawing of an empty tray. Draw the things that you think the teddy bears brought to share for their picnic. After you have done this you can colour the picture."

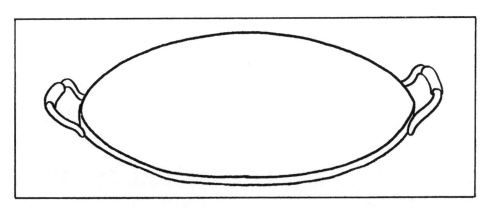

The Teddy Bears' Picnic

It was Saturday morning.

"Linda's not telling me things," complained Leroy. "She's sad and she's crying a bit. I keep on asking her what's wrong and all she says is, 'I'm not telling you, I'm only talking to my teddy'."

Leroy looked at his dad and his eyes filled with tears.

"It's not fair, daddy. It's not fair. Linda should tell me things. I'm her twin. She should tell me everything."

Josh could tell that his little son was very upset.

"Where is Linda?" he asked.

"In the hallway, that's where she is and she's sitting on the floor hiding underneath the hallstand just talking to her teddy and not to me," wailed Leroy.

Josh was trying to read his newspaper. He was sitting in his armchair.

"Oh! Dear me", said Josh as he pulled himself from his chair. "I suppose I had better go to see what's wrong with Linda."

He went into the hallway, and just as Leroy had said, there was Linda, sitting on the floor under the hallstand. She was clutching her teddy bear.

Josh bent down and lifted his little daughter into his arms. He carried her into the living room and sat her down next to him on the settee. Leroy joined them. The three of them were sitting on the settee. Linda was still holding her teddy.

Josh didn't say anything.

Leroy didn't say anything.

Linda didn't say anything.

After a short while, Josh said, "I wonder if teddy wants to tell me why Linda is sad?"

Linda didn't speak.

Leroy didn't speak.

Daddy didn't speak.

And teddy didn't speak.

Then daddy said, "Perhaps teddy wants to whisper something to me."

Linda looked at her teddy, and in a hushed voice whispered, "Tell daddy I'm sad because Paul's mummy is in hospital, and now he hasn't got a mummy."

Paul, who lived next door to Leroy and Linda, was sad because his mummy was in hospital, and Linda was sad because her friend was sad.

"Paul will be going to visit his mummy in hospital today", said Josh hugging his little daughter. "Would you and Leroy like to go to visit her too?"

"Only if I can bring teddy," answered Linda.

"Yes, and I will bring my teddy too," said Leroy.

That afternoon, Josh, Leroy, Linda and two teddy bears set off to go to the hospital.

Josh was carrying some cakes that he had made. He had also bought a bunch of flowers for Paul's mummy.

When they got to the hospital they asked a nurse to tell them which ward Sylvia was in. They found her bed.

"What a lovely surprise," said Sylvia, when she saw her visitors. She was sitting up in her bed and she looked very well. She was laughing and talking to Paul and to Steve, her husband.

"Why are you in hospital?" asked Linda.

"Because I have very high blood pressure," said Sylvia.

"But she is also going to have a new kidney one day," answered Paul, very seriously and continued, "When she gets one she can be at home all the time."

"Do you have to wait a long time for one to come?" asked Leroy.

Everybody laughed at that.

"When one comes, I will have to have an operation," explained Sylvia. "After a while I will come back home and then I won't have to keep coming to hospital for treatment."

Linda looked at Sylvia and then she looked at her teddy.

"I told you that Paul had got a mummy really," she whispered into her teddy's ear.

Leroy looked at his teddy and whispered rather loudly, "Ask Sylvia if she likes cakes to eat, because I do and I'm hungry."

Everybody laughed again.

Josh went to find a large tray. He asked a nurse if he could borrow one. Then he went to the drinks machine. He put the right money into the machine and bought three cups of tea. Next he put the right money into the machine for three cups of juice.

"Now for the cakes," he said, and put all the cakes onto the large tray.

There were lots of cakes and Sylvia said, "I can't have one but shall we ask the nurse if the other patients would like a cake to eat? We often share things."

So Leroy, Linda and Paul and a nurse took the tray round to the other patients and offered them a cake.

"Do you share all your things?" asked Leroy.

"Yes, they do" Paul answered, very knowingly. "They even share secrets."

"I sometimes share secrets with my teddy," said Linda.

"And so do I," chirped Leroy. "Then our teddies tell each other what we have said", he shouted very cheekily. He put the tray of cakes onto Sylvia's bed and placed the two teddy bears next to the tray.

"Goodness me," said the nurse who was coming to take Sylvia's temperature. "It looks like a teddy bears' picnic in here."

"It is," shouted all the children.

That night, before she went to sleep, Linda whispered to her teddy. "It's alright, Paul has got a mummy really, so you needn't be sad."

Leroy looked at his sister and said, "And my teddy is not sad either, but he has just told me that when Sylvia comes back home he wants another teddy bears' picnic."

Then the two children fell fast asleep.

Lesson 8: November

Story: **The Monster**
Theme: **The Unknown**

Synopsis

Leroy and Linda ask who lives at the Mystery House. Is it a monster? They decide to tempt him with good things to eat and drink, but after frightening and exciting times they discover that there are no monsters, just fat and very happy kittens.

Objectives

- To recognise what is right and wrong.

- To share opinions and explain their views.

- To recognise, name and deal with their feelings in a positive way.

- To think about themselves and learn from their experiences.

- To take part in discussions.

- To think about rules for and ways of keeping safe.

Preparing for the story

The teacher gathers the children on the carpet and tells them that firstly he is going to read two poems:

'Sometimes, when in bed, I find Scary monsters in my mind, And so I give myself a shake And make myself come wide awake. For I know there's nothing there Except for me and teddy bear.'	'Some people think there are witches. Some people think there are ghosts. Some people think there are monsters Wearing long prickly coats. Some people believe silly notions, But they should be told straight away, Many things are not real but just stories, We all can make up any day.'

The teacher has two sheets of paper which he displays to the children. The children sit on the carpet where they can see the lists. On one list the teacher writes the caption 'Things that are real'. On the other list the teacher writes 'Things that are not real' then explains that there are things which are real like tables and chairs and little black kittens. He writes this on the 'Things that are real' list and continues to say there are things that are not real like ghosts or monsters putting them on the 'Things that are not real' list. The teacher asks for other examples to be given by the children and then writes them on the appropriate list.

Here are some things which the children might suggest:

PSHE
2a.

English 1.
1 a, b, c. 2a, c, d.
3a, c.

Real: Members of family, food or drink, pets and other animals, toys etc.

Not Real: Monsters, giants, fairies, trolls, elves, gnomes, dragons, Superman, Spiderman etc.

The teacher can display the lists together with illustrations which the children can do at a later date.

Read the story

After the above activity has been completed the teacher reads the story to the children.

Circle Time discussion

PSHE
1c. 2a.

English 1.
1a, b, c. 2a, c, d.
3a, c.

Question 1 How do you think Leroy and Linda felt when they went to the Mystery House to leave food for the monster?

Would Leroy and Linda have felt frightened? Would they have been scared? Would they have been excited? Might they have been worried? If so why?

PSHE
2a. 3g.

English 1.
1a, b, c. 2a, c. d.
3a, c.

Question 2 Was it a sensible idea to investigate the Mystery House? If so why?

Was it a safe thing to do? Is it safe to go into someone else's garden? Were Leroy and Linda silly or sensible? Did they tell their mummy what they were doing? Did they tell the whole truth to their mummy? What might mummy have said if she had heard the whole story?

Question 3 Did Linda believe Leroy when he said a monster lived at the Mystery House or when he said he had seen the monster in the night?

PSHE
la. 2a.

English I.
la, b, c. 2a, c, d.
3a, c.

Did Leroy really believe that a monster lived at the Mystery House? Did Leroy really see the monster in the night? Do you think Leroy half believed his untruths?

Question 4 Who or what ate the food in the Mystery House?

PSHE
la. 2a.

English I.
la, b, c. 2a, c, d.
3a, c.

Were Leroy and Linda right or wrong to put the food there? Was it a good idea to put the food in the garden? Should you leave food on a paper plate or drink in a bottle in a garden which is not yours?

Question 5 Do you think that Leroy and Linda were relieved that it was the little black kitten and not the monster that stole their food?

PSHE
I c.

English I.
la, b, c. 2a, c, d.
3a, c.

Is there such a thing as a monster? Have you ever felt relieved about anything?

Question 6 Leroy and Linda were frightened about the Mystery House and monsters. What frightens you?

PSHE
I c. 2a.

English I.
la, b, c. 2a, c, d.
3a, c.

What are you scared of? Have you ever been frightened by a television programme or a story? Do real things frighten you? Do unreal things frighten you?

Supplementary ideas

The children are arranged in groups of four for an art lesson. Each group is given two pieces of paper, paints and different sized brushes. The teacher tells the children that they are going to paint two pictures. On one sheet of paper the children will paint something which is real: something of which they are not frightened like an apple, a chair or a person. On the other piece of paper the children will paint something that is not real, like a monster, ghost or fairy, and which they consider to be frightening. When the work is completed the teacher can make a large frieze or class book of things that are real and not real. He can add captions like:

'Monsters are only found in stories.'
'Here is a real person.'
'Susie painted a pretend ghost.'
'Sammy painted a tree which you can see in your garden.'

PSHE
1c.

Art & Design
1a.

The teacher gathers the children on the mat and reads the following poem:

'Here is a Mystery House, empty and bare,
No one goes near it, no one would dare.
No mail and no papers, nothing at all,
But boarded up windows and a cold, cold, wall.
Here is a roof on my house, painted red.
Here is my own chair and here is my bed,
Curtained windows, lights that shine,
My cat at the door, black gleaming and fine.'

The children are invited to say what their own house is like and what the Mystery House was like. The teacher has two boxes on which he can draw and put in doll's-house furniture and his own arte-facts which he has constructed previously. He builds two houses, an inhabited house and a Mystery House. The teacher will be guided by what the children say. There are two lists below of items which the children might suggest.

PSHE
1b, c. 2a, g.

My house	The Mystery House
Bed, cooker, fridge, sink, carpets. New number and name. Lamps and lights. People and animals. Television, settee, chairs, toy box, cupboards, sideboard.	Floorboards. Insects, spiders and cobwebs. Boarded up doors and windows. Broken furniture and litter. Old and broken name and number.

The teacher asks the children which house they would like to live in and why. Is one house scary and uninviting, cold and damp? Is another house warm friendly and inviting?

The teacher will provide each child with a zigzag book in the shape of a monster. The teacher can make these by making a concertina shaped zigzag book. When the book is closed the teacher cuts out a monster. On each page the child will draw a monster who is exhib-iting different emotions. The child can write underneath a model written by the teacher or helper. For example, my monster is happy, sad, angry, shy or frightened

Before the children start on this exercise the teacher should discuss with the children the emotions which their monsters might be feeling. The teacher may find it advantageous to have made his own monster book previously and show it to the children as an example of the finished product.

PSHE
1 d.

English 3.
1 2

The teacher reads to the class *The Gruffalo* by Julia Donaldson and Axel Scheffer and published by Macmillan. After reading the book the teacher asks the child if there is any such thing as a ghost, a witch, or a tree, or a frog etc. The children are read the following rhyming couplets by the teacher and asked to supply the rhyming word.

"I'll tell you this while eating my toast,
There's no such thing as a snow white ... (ghost)

I'll tell you something that isn't scary,
There's no such thing as a dancing ... (fairy)

Here is something I know myself,
There's no such thing as a giant or ... (elf)

You can look south or west or east.
There's no such thing as a blue hairy ... (beast)

English 3.
1 c.

Worksheet instructions

"On your worksheet you will find a picture of a person and an animal but they need a head. Will you make your person and your animal real or unreal? You choose what your person or animal will look like. After you have drawn a full person and a full animal you should colour in the picture."

The Monster

Leroy and Linda were talking quietly together.

"Who do you think lives in the Mystery House, Leroy?" asked Linda. "Do you think it is empty?"

"I think it is a monster that lives there," answered Leroy. "And it's a strange monster with six extra eyes. He see everything you know!"

Linda was a bit scared but she tried not to show it.

"I don't think so," said Linda sensibly. "I really think it is an empty house."

Then she added, "Maybe sometimes a tramp lives there."

"No way," said Leroy. "Sometimes, at night, I think I can hear him stamping about and shouting, 'I'm hungry'."

"I don't believe you," Linda said. "Let's go over to the Mystery House and have a look."

"But he never comes out in the daytime so you won't see him now," Leroy replied.

"Well, I'm still going to look," said Linda and went out of the house then down the garden path on her way to the Mystery House. Leroy followed his sister.

They stood on the pavement just outside the gate of the Mystery House. The house looked as if it held a secret for the doors and windows were boarded up.

The two children stood still. They were staring at the boarded up house and listening for any noise.

"Hello!" said a deep voice. "What are you two looking at?"

Leroy and Linda jumped. But the voice was not coming from the Mystery House. It was coming from behind them. It was Ronnie who was returning from Mr. Allsorts' shop. He had been to buy his newspaper. Ronnie was in his electric wheelchair. Neither Linda nor Leroy had heard him coming.

"Oh! Ronnie, you made us jump," said Linda. "We want to know about the Mystery House. Do you know anything about it?"

"Well, I might do," answered Ronnie, "but there's Matti and I want a word with her." He pointed over to the building opposite, which was Morningdale Court.

So the two children were no wiser.

"If the monster is hungry, he will come out at the dead of night looking for something to eat," said Leroy. "So I think that we should leave a big fat sandwich for him on a plate in the garden of the Mystery House and a bottle of orange juice as well. Then if tomorrow the food and drink have gone we will know that the monster came out at night time and had a good feast."

"Yes," laughed Linda rather excitedly. "We will ask mummy for a picnic tea, and ask her to make us lots of big fat sandwiches."

"And two plastic bottles of orange juice, too," added Leroy.

It was a nice day and Brenda, the twins' mummy, said 'yes' the twins could have a picnic tea. She didn't know that the twins were going over to the Mystery House and that they were going to leave a big sandwich in the garden. Mummy didn't know that the twins were going to share one bottle of orange juice and leave the other one in the garden of the Mystery House.

"If a monster with eight eyes lives here he will easily see the big sandwich and the drink," said Leroy, as he and Linda crept into the garden of the Mystery House. They put a big meat paste sandwich on a paper plate and left it near the doorstep. Then they took a bottle of orange juice from their little picnic basket and a plastic cup and left those on the doorstep of the Mystery House.

"Monster, monster, here's something to eat,

Monster, monster, we've brought you a treat,

Monster, monster, eat it and drink it all up,

Monster, monster, we've brought you a cup," sang Leroy, who was good at making up rhymes.

Then the twins ran away laughing and ate their own picnic tea in their back garden, which was far away from the monster with eight eyes.

For a while they forgot about what they had done but at night-time they found it hard to get to sleep and then when they did they kept waking up. Each time they awoke they crept to their bedroom window to see if they could see the Monster having a midnight feast.

The moon was shining and the stars were twinkling but each time the twins looked out of their window they saw nothing.

But the next morning Leroy told Linda that he had looked when she was fast asleep and that he had definitely seen the monster with eight eyes and it had waved to him with its long, long, arms.

"Oh! No, you didn't," said Linda.

"Yes, I DID," protested Leroy.

"Well then, I am going over to the Mystery House to see if the sandwich and the drink have gone," Linda answered.

Leroy was quiet. He didn't know what to say, but he followed Linda out of the house and across the green and over to the Mystery House.

The two children crept past the gate. They were whispering. Then when they looked at the paper plate they discovered it was empty and the bottle of orange juice had been knocked over.

"There you are, see, there really is a monster and he's eaten the sandwich and I think he was just going to have his drink of orange juice when he saw us coming and now he's gone away to hide again," yelled Leroy.

"Is he a shy monster?" asked Linda, who thought that Leroy must be right and that he had seen a monster when she was fast asleep.

Shama, who was in her garden, had seen the twins going into the garden of the Mystery House, and she could hear what they were saying.

"So, that is where you got this big fat sandwich from," she said to her kitten who was busily tucking into a very good meal.

For a moment Shama thought of saying nothing to the twins but then she thought again.

"It is not very nice to think that monsters really exist, is it?" she said to her kitten, "I will go and tell Leroy and Linda that it is you who is eating their sandwich."

Shama walked down The Crescent to the Mystery House.

"There are no monsters," said Shama to Leroy and Linda. "There are no monsters with eight eyes but I know one little monster who is busily eating your sandwich at this very moment and that is my little black kitten. He is in my garden and is having a lovely feast."

Then Linda smiled.

Next Leroy smiled.

And Shama smiled.

The twins followed Shama into her garden and saw the little black kitten, who also seemed to smile and started to purr.

"There are no monsters, Leroy and Linda, only very fat and very happy black kittens."

Lesson 9: December

> **Story:** The Christmas Cards
> **Theme:** Play and Creativity

Synopsis

Leroy and Linda make a mistake. They think 'Victoria Sponge' is a person, not a cake, and they decide to make her a Christmas card. The story concerns itself with the creative act and how to cope with derision. Mum (Brenda) and Dad (Josh) comfort the twins and praise the creativity of the young pair.

Objectives

- To recognise what is fair and unfair.

- To recognise name and deal with their feelings in a positive way.

- To learn from their experiences.

- To take part in discussion.

- To realise that others have needs and they have responsibilities to meet them.

- To learn that all household products can be harmful if not properly used.

Preparing for the story

The teacher collects some example cards - birthday, get well soon, thinking of you, retirement and celebrating religious festivals etc. She shows the cards to the children. The children guess what the cards celebrate by looking at the pictures and listening to the verse. The teacher gathers the children into groups of four. She gives them four cards, which have previously been cut into four or six pieces. The children have to re-assemble the jigsaw cards into four whole cards.

PSHE
4b. 5f.

Read the story

After the above activity has been completed the teacher reads the story to the children.

Circle Time discussion

PSHE
1a. 2a.

English 1.
1a, b, c. 2a, c, d.
3a, c.

Question 1 Leroy and Linda wanted to make a card for 'Victoria Sponge'. Was that a kind and fair thing to do?

Do you like to receive cards? Do you think that most people like cards? Had Leroy and Linda made cards for other people? If 'Victoria Sponge' had been a person might she have felt hurt and sad if Matti had got a card and Ronnie had got a card but she hadn't? Was it kind of Leroy and Linda to include 'Victoria Sponge'? Was it fair and friendly to make a card for 'Victoria Sponge'?

PSHE
1c. 2a.

English 1.
1a, b, c. 2a, c. d.
3a, c.

Question 2 When Linda and Leroy were making the card to send to 'Victoria Sponge' were they happy?

Have you ever made a card for someone? What sort of card was it? How did you feel when you were making the card? Linda had a 'card kit'; would it be nice to have the materials for making a card? Does making something sometimes make you feel happy?

PSHE
1b, c. 2a.

English 1.
1a, b, c. 2a, c, d.
3a, c.

Question 3 Leroy and Linda made a mistake, but did it matter?

Are mistakes important? Do you think that everyone makes mistakes? Were Leroy and Linda still being kind even though they made a mistake? If 'Victoria Sponge' had been a person do you think she would have appreciated a card and would it have made her happy?

PSHE
1b, c. 2a.

English 1.
1a, b, c. 2a, c, d.
3a, b, c.

Question 4 Was it helpful of Jenny to laugh at the twins' mistake?

Did the twins like or dislike it when Jenny laughed at them? Have you ever been laughed at? How did you feel?

Question 5 Was mummy kind to Leroy and Linda? What did she say?

PSHE
2a. 4d.

English 1.
1a, b, c. 2a, c, d.
3a, b, c.

Did she blame the twins for making a mistake? Whose mistake did she say that it was? Did mummy or daddy laugh at Leroy and Linda? Did mummy praise Linda and Leroy? Did she say they 'made her up out of their own minds'? Was that good?

Question 6 Imagine that you are making a card for a make believe person. Who is that person?

PSHE
2a. 4e.

English 1.
1a, b, c. 2a, c, d.
3a, c.

What is their name? If that person were real do you think it would make her/him happy? Do you think it is nice to make believe? Is it good to know what is real or unreal or what is fact and fiction? Is it nice to make up names? Do some of your toys have names which you have given them? Do we all need names? Why do we all need names? What else do real people need that imaginary people don't need? (food, shelter, warmth etc.) Are there some names that you like to be called? Are there some names which you do not like to be called? Can calling names be a nasty, bullying thing to do?

Supplementary ideas

The children are seated in groups of four. Each table has been provided with pens, pencils, paper, glue and collage materials. The teacher tells the children that Leroy and Linda made a Christmas card for an imaginary person but the children in class are going to make a card for a real person. They can make any sort of card they want. The card may be to celebrate a festival, or it may be a get well, thank you, retirement or new home card. The teacher tells the children to think who the card is for and to make sure that person would like the card. Teachers and adult helpers help each child to write the name of the person to and from whom the card will be sent.

PSHE
2c.
Art & Design
la.

Leroy and Linda's mum was making a cake. The children sit where they can all see the whiteboard, blackboard or writing display. The teacher writes the following list and draws a simple picture by it to act as an illustration.

Eggs	Sugar	Tablets
Medicine	Bread	Oranges
Flour	Milk	Glue
Disinfectant	Butter	Ointment
Potatoes	Bucket	Fish

The teacher asks the children which items they would use if they were making a cake. The teacher puts a tick against each correct ingredient. The teacher asks the children which items would be harmful if the children ate them. She colours these blue. The teacher asks the children which items would make a good healthy choice for a meal. She colours these red.

PSHE
3f.

The teacher tells the children that Leroy and Linda liked to help their mummy make cakes, and they enjoyed collage, and painting and drawing. The teacher asks the children what they do at home time. Volunteer children complete the sentence:

PSHE
la, b, d. 2a.

At home time I sometimes like to…

Worksheet instructions

"Someone has received a handmade card through their letter box. It has made that person very happy. Look at the worksheet - it shows a picture of a card and a door in alternate squares, or every other square. Now think of two things that you like and draw them alternately in the squares."

(The teacher might like to demonstrate a repeat pattern on the blackboard or whiteboard.)

"Now when you have finished your drawings colour in your pictures."

When completed the teacher may like to ask for volunteers to say what they have drawn, what makes them happy and why. The teacher could also make a huge card or cards for display purposes and she could glue the children's patterns on to four sides of the card.

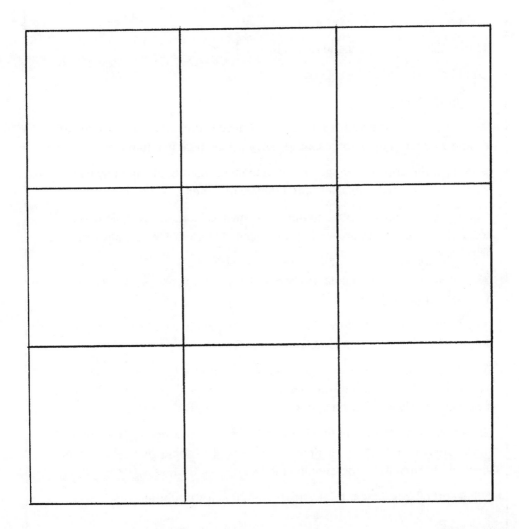

The Christmas Cards

When Ronnie and Matti came to Leroy and Linda's house for tea they saw two of the most beautiful Christmas cards you have ever seen. The cards were standing on the window ledge. They were big cards and they were handmade. The cards shone with gold and silver glitter and this is how they were made.

Leroy and Linda had just arrived home from school. Josh had been to collect them that day. Linda took her coat off and hung it neatly on her peg.

Leroy rushed into the kitchen to see what was happening. Mummy was very busy. She was making sandwiches and scones and the food mixer was whirring away.

"What are you doing?" Leroy asked.

"I am making the tea," said his mummy in a hurry.

"Can I help?" asked Leroy eagerly.

Mummy gave a sigh.

"Not now, Leroy" she said 'I'm in a hurry. I have invited Matti and Ronnie to tea and we're having Victoria sponge. They will be here in a minute."

Leroy took the drink of orange juice and the biscuits that his mummy had given him to his bedroom. He shared them with Linda.

"Linda," he said importantly, "mummy has invited Matti and Ronnie to our house for tea and another lady is coming called Victoria Sponge, have you heard of her?"

"No, I don't know her", Linda answered, "Do you think she is another lady from Morningdale Court?"

"I don't think so," said Leroy, "I know all of the people who live in Morningdale Court and not one of them is called Victoria Sponge."

"Well I think that we should make a Christmas card for her," said Linda, "We have made cards for Ronnie and we have made cards for Matti, so it is only fair if we make cards for Victoria Sponge."

Linda rushed downstairs to find her Christmas card making kit. There was shiny card and glitter and felt-tipped pens as well as some glue. All the things they needed to make cards were in Linda's kit.

"What sort of lady do you think she is?" asked Leroy doubtfully.

"I think she is magic and that she has long, curly hair and carries a magic wand," said Linda. "Yes", chirped Leroy, entering into the spirit of things, "Yes, she will have magic powers. Perhaps she will turn Hope, the dog, into a reindeer and then fly across the sky with Father Christmas."

Leroy and Linda both started to make their own cards for Victoria Sponge.

Leroy drew a magic wand and a picture of Father Christmas in the sky.

Linda drew a picture of a beautiful lady.

Leroy and Linda decorated their cards with shiny coloured paper shapes and glitter.

Inside the cards they each wrote a message.

To Viktoria Spung	To Vicorea Spooge
Happi Crismmas	Meri Xmas
Love from Leroy	Love from Linda

Just as they were finishing their cards, Jenny, their big sister arrived home.

Why were the twins so quiet she thought? They were usually making a big noise at that time of the day and rampaging all over the place.

She went upstairs to find Leroy and Linda.

"What are you doing?" she asked, curious to know why there was a hush about the house.

"We are both making a card for Victoria Sponge", said Leroy very importantly, "She is coming to our house for her tea you know."

Jenny could not believe her ears. "Victoria Sponge is not a person. It's a cake," she blurted out, and ran out of the room laughing. Jenny had to put her hand over her mouth because she was having a fit of the giggles.

Leroy looked at Linda and Linda looked at Leroy. What was wrong? What had they done to make Jenny laugh? They didn't understand.

Josh came into the twins' bedroom to explain to Leroy and Linda.

"It's a mistake that anybody could make" said Josh kindly.

"It is not your mistake it is mine," said their mummy, "After all it was me who didn't tell you that Victoria sponge is a cake and not a person's name. But you two did something that not many people can do. You made her up out of your own minds and you have made her two beautiful cards."

And that is how two of the best Christmas cards that were ever made came to be standing on the window ledge of Number 8 The Crescent.

Lesson 10: December

> **Story:** **The Glow in the Dark**
> **Theme:** **Darkness and Light**

Synopsis

Leroy and Linda find that darkness is alarming when there is a power cut and their lion light no longer shines. Adult intervention (partly in the guise of Sophie who is blind) calms the situation. The story deals with the comfort of light which shines in the darkness, the notion of blindness and the concept of the guide.

Objectives

- To recognise what is right and wrong.

- To recognise, name and deal with their feelings in a positive way.

- To take part in discussions.

- To realise that people and other living things have needs.

- To recognise people who can help them feel safe.

- To recognise how their behaviour affects other people.

- To play and work co-operatively.

- To identify and respect the differences and similarities between people.

- To know that family and friends should care for each other.

- To know there are different types of teasing and bullying and that it is wrong.

- To feel positive about themselves.

- To meet and talk with people.

Preparing for the story

The children sit on the carpet or where they can see a display board. The teacher brings in a blindfold and a large picture of a candle without a flame which is mounted on card. The large picture of the candle is displayed at the front. The teacher asks for a volunteer child to be blindfolded and to pin the flame on the candle. After the child has been blindfolded and the candle flame placed on the candle the initials of the child is placed on the card where he or she pinned the flame. The child's blindfold is removed and another volunteer is selected. After five volunteers have pinned the flame on the candle the game ends and the teacher points out to all the children where each volunteer has placed the flame. The teacher asks each volunteer how they felt when they were blindfolded and if it was difficult to guess where the picture of the candle was. Was it dark when they were blindfolded and is it light now? Is it more difficult to see in the dark than in the light? The teacher explains that some people are blind and cannot see. How best can we help them? Some blind people have a guide dog to help them.

PSHE
Ic. 2a, e. 4c.

English I.
Ia, b, c. 2a, c, d. 3a, c.

Art & Design
5c.

Read the story

After the above activity has been completed the teacher reads the story to the children.

Circle Time discussion

PSHE
Ic. 2a.

English I.
Ia, b, c. 2a, c, d. 3a, c.

Question I At the beginning of the story did the twins feel excited? Why did they feel excited?

Did they feel excited because it was Christmas? What else did the twins feel in the story? Were they frightened when there was a power cut? Did they feel happy when their landing light lion came back on?

PSHE
2a. 3g.

English I.
Ia, b, c. 2a, c. d. 3a, c.

Question 2 Who and what made Linda and Leroy feel safe?

Did the soft light from the landing light lion make Linda and Leroy feel safe? Did their daddy make them feel safe when the lights went out? How did he do this? Did Sophie and Hope and the candles they were delivering make the twins feel safe?

Question 3 Was it right for Leroy to play tricks on Linda and kick the tinsel out of her hand?

Could Leroy really do magic tricks? Did he really make it thunder? How would Linda feel if the tinsel was kicked out of her hand by Leroy? Has anyone ever played tricks on you? How did you feel? Was it fair or kind? Do you think Leroy was bullying Linda? Is it a right thing to do?

Question 4 Sophie was blind. What might this feel like?

What would you not be able to do if you were blind? What did Sophie do that was helpful to others in the story? Who guided her way? Do you think that guide dogs for the blind are a good idea? Why? Do you think Sophie was scared? Who helped her in the story?

Question 5 What might be helpful and unhelpful to a blind person? What would be right or wrong to do?

Would it be helpful to pat the guide dog when it is working? Would it be helpful or wrong to leave litter or obstructions on the pathway?

Question 6 Whose behaviour in the story affected other people?

Did Leroy's magic trick affect other people? Did Josh comfort Leroy and Linda? Did Sophie and Hope give light to other people?

Supplementary ideas

The children work in pairs with an adult helper. They shine a torch to make a silhouette picture of their face on black paper. The adult helper draws the reflected silhouette with white chalk or wax white crayon on the black paper. The child cuts out their own silhouette, with help if needed. The child's silhouette and name is put onto the black paper. The adult helper and the child mark down the child's achievements, interest and good qualities. For example, Amanda Brown has a medal for swimming and a certificate for never being late. She is kind and often smiling. She does good drawings and paintings and can write her name. This is displayed.

The teacher cuts out different shapes of white paper to represent candles. Each child is given a paper cut out and a candle. The children are instructed to press the candle down hard onto the paper to make a pattern which is wax resistant. With thinly mixed paint colour, the children wash the paper cut out to make a pattern. The teacher makes a frieze of the candles adding tissue or foil to make a

PSHE
1a. 2a. 4e.

English 1.
1a, b, c. 2a, c. d.
3a, c.

PSHE
2a. 4c, d.

English 1.
1a, b, c. 2a, c, d.
3a, c.

PSHE
1a. 2a.

English 1.
1a, c. 2a, c, d.
3a, c.

PSHE
2a. 4a.

English 1.
1a, b, c. 2a, c, d.
3a, c.

PSHE
1d. 2a. 5b.

PSHE
5b.

Art & Design
5c.

flame for each candle. An appropriate caption is added to the frieze such as 'Let your light shine' or 'A candle brightens the darkness and shows us the way'.

PSHE
2a, e. 5e.

English 1.
2a, e.

The teacher can invite a person who is blind to come and speak to the children. Suitable topics for a talk could be:

'How my guide dog helps me.'

'What I find helpful or unhelpful.'

The children should be encouraged to ask appropriate questions.

The children and teacher gather in the hall. A child volunteer is blindfolded and another volunteer child leads his partner through soft obstacles. When all volunteers have enjoyed their turn the teacher asks the following questions:

- What was it like to be led?

- How might daily living be difficult for a blind person?

PSHE
4a, b, c, d.

- How did you feel when you were blindfolded or were being led?

- What was helpful when you were blindfolded?

- What did you find difficult or hard to do when you were blindfolded?

Worksheet instructions

"On your worksheets are two patterns. They are made as if you were looking through a kaleidoscope. Colour the patterns in colours of your own choosing. Do you like the pattern? How would it be for a person who was blind? Would they have to rely on words if they wanted to know what the pattern was like?"

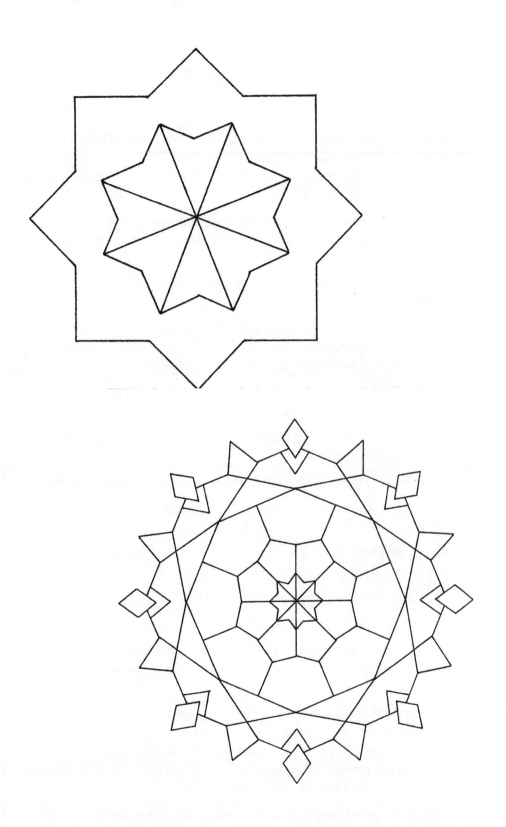

Lesson 10

The Glow in the Dark

Leroy and Linda had been told four times to go to bed but they hadn't listened. They were very excited. The Christmas holidays had just begun. Josh was busy putting the lights on the Christmas tree and Jenny and her mummy were making cakes and decorations.

"I can do magic," shouted Leroy. He was wearing his glow-in-the-dark pyjamas. These pyjamas were decorated with kittens and the kitten's eyes glowed in the dark.

"No you can't," said Linda very bossily. She too was wearing glow-in-the-dark pyjamas. She was carrying a little box of silver tinsel strips over to the Christmas tree.

The Christmas tree was in the front room, and Josh said that it would look very pretty standing in front of the window.

"It will light up our garden path and Santa Claus will be able to see where Number 8 The Crescent is," Jenny had told the twins.

"Yes, I can do magic, watch me," insisted Leroy and he kicked the box of tinsel strips out of Linda's hands.

"That's snow," he yelled excitedly, as the silver tinsel strips flew everywhere.

Linda was very cross with her brother and told him that all he could do was silly magic.

But Leroy still jumped up and down and carried on shouting about all the magic tricks he could do.

Then he pushed the living room door. It closed with a loud bang.

"That's thunder, that's thunder," he shrieked, "I've made it thunder."

The sudden noise frightened Linda and she rushed out of the room saying that she was going to sleep on the spare bed in Jenny's room and not in the same room as Leroy.

She was very pleased that the landing light lamp was switched on. This little lamp had been given to the twins for their birthday. It was in the shape of a little lion, and the twins called it the landing light lion. From this lamp a soft light shone into the twins' bedroom and made them feel safe at night. Neither Linda nor Leroy liked the dark.

Linda went into Jenny's bedroom and closed the door with a bang.

After a few minutes she heard Leroy run upstairs and close his bedroom door with a bang.

Then Leroy opened his bedroom door a little bit and Linda opened her door a little bit.

Linda could see the light from the landing lion lamp.

Leroy could see the light from the landing lion lamp.

Linda snuggled down in her bed.

Leroy snuggled down in his bed.

Leroy thought about the twinkling lights on the Christmas tree. He told himself they were magic lights.

Linda thought about the twinkling lights on the Christmas tree. She told herself they were fairyland lights.

Then suddenly a terrible thing happened. All the lights went out. The Christmas tree lights went out. The kitchen light went out. The light in the street went out. But worst of all the landing lamp lion went out.

"Leroy, where are you?" screamed Linda, "don't do any more magic tricks."

"Linda, where are you?" screamed Leroy, "I can't do magic tricks, it's not me."

"Stop those silly magic tricks," called their mummy. "Josh, is it you being silly, I am trying to make some cakes and I can't see a thing," she shouted crossly.

"Nobody is doing magic tricks," shouted Josh. "It's a power cut."

"I don't like the dark," wailed Leroy.

"I don't like the dark," wailed Linda.

Both children jumped out of their beds and fell onto the landing.

"Stay where you are," called their daddy. "I am coming to get you."

Josh could see his children. They were both wearing their glow-in-the-dark pyjamas.

The light from the moon and the stars shone through the landing window.

"Everything is alright, calm down," said Josh. "It's only a power cut."

Leroy looked through the window.

"Who's that?" he screamed. "Who's that in The Crescent?"

Linda looked through the window. She could see somebody dressed in a long cloak.

"It's Father Christmas with Rudolph and he won't be able to find our house in the dark," howled Linda.

"No, it's not," said Josh kindly. "It's Sophie, and she is taking Hope, her guide dog, for a walk."

It was Sophie and it was Hope, her guide dog, and Paul's dad was also there.

They were delivering candles to all the houses in The Crescent.

Very soon all the houses were lit with candlelight, and the stars and the moon shone brightly in the sky. Everything looked very magical in The Crescent because there were so many beautiful flickering lights.

Sophie knocked on the door of Number 8 The Crescent, and before long all the neighbours were together in Leroy and Linda's house drinking hot chocolate made on a calor gas stove by candlelight.

Linda was very quiet and after a short while she spoke.

"Is it always dark for you, Sophie?" asked Linda.

"Oh no!" said Sophie. "I can tell when it is dark and I can tell when it is light, but I always have Hope to guide me."

Hope stood up, pulled on her lead and gave a little bark.

"I think Hope is trying to tell me something," said Sophie. And she was. For just at that second all the lights came on again and everybody shouted Hooray!

"Hope can always see Sophie, can't she daddy?" asked Leroy, "because dogs can see in the dark."

"Yes," said Josh, who was tucking the children into their beds, "and even if it's dark I can see Leroy and Linda because they are both wearing glow in the dark pyjamas."

"Put the light out, daddy," said Linda, "I can do magic, I can see Leroy in the dark."

And the two children laughed.

"I'm not scared of the dark any more," said Leroy.

"I'm not scared of the dark anymore," said Linda. "But will you leave our bedroom door open a little bit so that we can see the landing light lion?"

Josh did leave the door open a little bit. The lion glowed and a soft ray of light shone into Leroy and Linda's bedroom. A few minutes later the two little children were fast asleep.

Lesson 11: January

> **Story:** **The Sad Happening**
> **Theme:** **Loss, Rejection and Identification**

Synopsis

Everybody was sad when Rosie lost Danny Bear and they helped her to search for her lost treasure. The story shows how searching is a part of grieving and that the act of mutual comforting helps to heal a wound. The tale acts as a gentle introduction to the concept of loss.

Objectives

- To recognise, name and deal with feelings in a positive way.

- To take part in discussion.

- To realise that other people have needs and they have responsibilities to meet them.

- To understand that they belong to various groups and communities.

- To know that family and friends should care for each other.

- To understand that sometimes loss cannot be rectified but is permanent.

- To begin to think of effective ways to comfort another in need.

Preparing for the story

The children go into the hall. They all find a space and close their eyes. The teacher hides three teddy bears. The children are told by the teacher to open their eyes. They are then asked to find the bears. They are asked to do this three times. On the fourth occasion another adult is asked to take the bears to the classroom. The children search and search but cannot find the bears. Then the teacher says that the game is over. Each child sits in a space. The teacher asks the question, "How did you feel when you could not find the bear?" and volunteer children are asked to answer this question.

PSHE
1c.

Read the story

After the above activity has been completed the teacher reads the story to the children.

Circle Time discussion

PSHE
4d.

English I.
I a, b, c. 2a, c, d.
3a, c.

Question I Who helped Rosie look for her Danny Bear and was that a helpful thing to do?

Did Leroy and Linda, Josh and Big Dan care about Rosie losing her Danny Bear? Was searching for Danny Bear a right thing to do even though Danny Bear was never found?

PSHE
I c.

English I.
I a, b, c. 2a, c. d.
3a, e.

Question 2 Was everybody sad when Rosie lost her Danny Bear?

Did Rosie cry when she couldn't find her Danny Bear? If someone cries do we know that they are sad? Did everyone feel sad about the lost bear? Was it easy to imagine how Rosie must have been feeling?

Question 3 How did people try to comfort Rosie because she had lost her bear and do you think that helped Rosie?

PSHE
2a. 4d.

English I.
I a, b, c. 2a, c. d.
3a, b, c, d, e.

Do you think that everyone looking for Danny Bear helped Rosie to feel better? Was it a kind thing to do? Did Leroy say they would have to look after Rosie and give her lots of hugs? Do you think that receiving cards helped Rosie? Do you think she was glad because she had such good friends?

PSHE
I c. 2a.

English I.
I a, b, c. 2a, c, d.
3a, e.

Question 4 Does losing things make you feel sad?

Have you ever lost anything? Did you search for it? Does it make you feel sad if you lose something? Do you always find things that are lost?

Question 5 Why was Big Dan upset?

PSHE
2a. 4d.

English I.
I a, b, c. 2a, c, d.
3a, c.

Did Big Dan remember being a little boy? Do you think he might have lost something when he was a little boy? Who in the story tried to comfort Big Dan? Do you think that it helped Rosie to feel better when she comforted Big Dan? Do grown-up people sometimes get upset?

124

Question 6 Big Dan said it was nice to have good friends. Do you think so?

Who is your friend? Why? Did Big Dan have lots of friends? Does a good friend try to help you when things go wrong? Do good friends comfort you if you have lost something? How do they comfort you? Can you think of a good way to comfort someone who had lost something important to them? Does everyone sometimes lose something?

PSHE
1b. 2a, e, f. 4d.

English 1.
1a, b, c. 2a, c, d. 3a, c.

Supplementary ideas

The teacher sits all the children round on the carpet and asks them if they can think of a time when everyone was happy together. Perhaps the children remember a day out together or a holiday together. The children then go to their places. They each have a sheet of paper and the teacher tells them that they are going to draw a picture where everyone is happy. When the pictures are finished they can be discussed. The teacher asks the children if they like it when everyone is happy. Does it make them feel even more happy? Does it work the same for other emotions? Do we feel more sad if everyone is sad?

PSHE
1c. 2a.

The teacher sits the children on the carpet and shows them her ready prepared sheet of paper. On the paper are things that would make a person happy or sad. The teacher draws a glum face if the item makes the children feel sad and a smiley face if the item makes the children feel happy. The following is a list of suggestions:

- You have just lost your favourite toy and cannot find it again.
- Your favourite person is coming to your house for tea.
- You go to a café and have your favourite food and drink.
- A special friend is not well.
- Today at school it is your best lesson.
- It is your birthday and you have just got a new toy.
- You want to go out to play but it is raining.
- Your friend gives you a hug.
- Someone special sends you a card.
- The postman goes past your house and does not bring a letter.
- Everyone is too busy to take you to the recreation ground.
- A good friend of yours is sad.

PSHE

Ic.

- A good friend of yours is happy.

- You have caught an illness.

- Someone tripped you up in the playground.

The children sit on the carpet with the teacher. The teacher asks the children what makes them sad and what makes them happy. Together the children think of some way to finish these sentences. The teacher writes an example of each sentence on the whiteboard or blackboard for the children to read back.

PSHE

Ic. 2a.

English 2.

If.

'I feel happy when…'

'1 feel sad when…'

'My friends are…'

'Some people who help me are…'

'Sometimes things make me cry because…'

'Sometimes I laugh because…'

Worksheet instructions

"On the big picture are three objects or things hiding in the wiggly lines. Can you find Big Dan, Rosie and a teddy bear?"

(The teacher or other adult helper ascertains that each child can find the objects.)

"Now colour them in.

On the second worksheet a wiggly line has been started. Can you carry on the wiggly line? Do not scribble, just draw a bendy line until you fill the circle. Now see if you can see anything in your picture and colour it in. I can already see a balloon - can you?"

The Sad Happening

Leroy and Linda had a friend called Rosie. Rosie was in the same class at school as Leroy and Linda. Rosie did not live in The Crescent but she did live in the same town.

One Saturday morning in December Josh said to Leroy and Linda,

"Would you like to come with me to the recreation ground? I am going to help Big Dan. He is collecting wood for the bonfire we are having on New Year's Day."

"Wow, yes please," shouted the twins.

"I want my friend Rosie to come too," said Linda.

"Yes, and I want Rosie to come with us and I want Ben to come as well," said Leroy.

Ben was another of Leroy and Linda's friends from school. Ben did not live in The Crescent, but he did live in the same town as Leroy and Linda.

"Alright," said Josh, "we will go to Rosie's house and ask if she can come with us, and then we will go to Ben's house and ask if he can come with us too."

Very soon they were all on the recreation ground.

"Hello! Big Dan," shouted Josh, "we have all come to help you."

"Hello! Big Dan," laughed Leroy.

"Hello! Big Dan," shouted Linda.

"Hello! Big Dan," shouted Ben.

"Hello! Big Dan," laughed Rosie, "I've come to help you too and look whom I have brought. I have brought Danny Bear. Do you remember him?"

Big Dan did remember Rosie's teddy bear because she had won it at the fair which was held on the recreation ground each year. Big Dan was the one who had given Rosie her prize. He was the man who was in charge of everything that happened on the recreation ground.

All the children in Riley Green knew Big Dan and all the children liked him. He was good fun.

"I call him Danny Bear," laughed Rosie.

"Yes, she calls him Danny Bear after you," Linda added.

"That is why she calls him Danny Bear," said Leroy rather importantly. "It is because it is your name and you gave her the prize."

All the children laughed and jumped up and down. They were very happy.

Many people had come to the recreation ground to help Big Dan build the bonfire.

It was going to be the best bonfire ever.

At the end of that day all the children were very tired. They had been working hard collecting wood for the bonfire, which had grown so big.

"The bonfire is nearly as tall as my house," said Leroy.

"And it's even bigger than Big Dan," said Linda.

It was while Rosie was getting ready for bed that she noticed Danny Bear was missing.

"Oh No!" she cried, "I have left Danny Bear on the recreation ground."

Rosie's mummy came to look to see if she could find Danny Bear in Rosie's bedroom.

She couldn't find Danny Bear.

Rosie's daddy came to see if he could find Danny Bear in Rosie's bedroom.

He couldn't find Danny Bear.

Rosie's brother came to see if he could find Danny Bear in Rosie's bedroom.

Freddie couldn't find Danny Bear.

Danny Bear was not there.

Rosie was very sad.

"We will have to go back to the recreation ground," said Rosie's daddy.

So Rosie and her mummy and daddy and her brother Freddie all went back to the recreation ground.

Big Dan was still there and so were Josh and Leroy and Linda.

"I have lost Danny Bear," cried Rosie. "I have left him somewhere."

Poor Rosie began to cry and all the people felt very sorry for Rosie. Everybody began to look for Danny Bear but he was nowhere to be found.

"I want Danny Bear to come back," cried Linda.

"I want Danny Bear to come back," cried Leroy.

"I want my Danny Bear to come back," cried Rosie.

"Danny Bear is lost. He is nowhere to be found," said Josh, who looked all over the recreation ground.

"Oh! dear," said Rosie's mummy.

"Oh! dear," said Rosie's daddy.

"Oh! dear," said Freddie.

"That's very sad for Rosie," cried Linda, and she gave her friend a big hug.

"It's sad for me too," cried Leroy, and he went over to Rosie and put his arms round her.

Big Dan looked very sad as well.

"We will have to see if you can win another teddy bear the next time the fair comes to the recreation ground," he said.

"I don't want another teddy bear. I just want my Danny Bear," Rosie sobbed. "He was the best teddy bear that ever lived."

Poor Linda and Leroy didn't know what to do.

"We will have to look after Rosie now," said Linda.

"Yes, we will have to love her very much and help her," said Leroy, "and give her lots of hugs."

Big Dan looked at the children and he too began to cry. A big tear rolled down his cheek.

"Oh! dear," sobbed Dan because all the children rushed over to hug Big Dan.

"What's the matter, Big Dan?" asked Rosie.

"What's the matter, Big Dan?" asked Leroy.

"What's the matter, Big Dan?" asked Linda.

But Big Dan could not speak.

"I think Big Dan must have lost something very special to him when he was a little boy," said Leroy.

"Yes, and that is why he is crying," said Linda.

"Did you lose something very special when you were a little boy?" asked Rosie.

Big Dan nodded his head and said yes he did.

Rosie gave Big Dan an even bigger hug because he really understood just how much she missed her Danny Bear.

The next day Leroy and Linda each made a card for Rosie and they each made a card for Big Dan.

Rosie thought it was very kind and she said she was glad she had such good friends.

Big Dan said he would always keep his cards that the children had sent him and he said he was very glad that the children were his friends.

Lesson 12: January

Story: The Guinea Pigs
Theme: Thoughts and Promises

Synopsis

This theme deals with the care of animals. The story concerns itself with Leroy and Linda and how they failed to keep their promise to their new pets, and what happens as a consequence.

Objectives

- To recognise what they like, what is fair and unfair and what is right and wrong.

- To share opinions on things that matter to them and take part in discussions.

- To realise that other living things have needs and they have responsibilities to meet them.

- To know that medicines can be harmful if not used properly.

- To identify and respect the differences between people.

- To know that family and friends should care for each other.

- To know that bullying and hitting others is wrong.

- To have the opportunity to listen to others talk.

Preparing for the story

The teacher gathers the children on the carpet. He has a list written on a large sheet of paper, which he displays to the children explaining that the list contains promises made by members of the school.

Promises at our School

The teacher	I promise to polish the floors
The headteacher	I promise to lock the doors every night
The caretaker	I promise to teach the children
The school secretary	I promised to take assembly
The cleaner	I promised to type the holiday list.

PSHE
2a. 4d.

The children's task is to match the promises to the appropriate people. The teacher reads one promise and then the list of people. He asks the children which is the correct choice. The teacher then draws a line to match the promise to the person.

Read the story

After the above activity has been completed the teacher reads the story to the children.

Circle Time discussion

PSHE
1a. 2a.

English 1.
1a, b, c. 2a, c, d.
3a, c.

Question 1 Was it right or wrong that Leroy and Linda stopped looking after their guinea pigs?

Was it right or wrong that the twins should break their promise? Why? Did the guinea pigs need someone to look after them? Do you think that Shama would look after the guinea pigs properly?

PSHE
1a. 2a, c. 4e.

English 1.
1a, b, c. 2a, c, d.
3a, c.

Question 2 Had Jenny made any promises? Should the twins have hit Jenny?

Was it right or wrong for the twins to say that Jenny was to blame for their loss? Was hitting her fair and right or was it unfair and wrong?

PSHE
2a, e.

English 1.
1a, b, c. 2a, c. d.
3a, c.

Question 3 What things did the guinea pigs need?

Were the guinea pigs alive? Are toys alive? Do living things need care and attention? Did the guinea pigs need a hutch and food and water every day? Did the twins promise to clean out the hutch? Did they?

PSHE
1b. 2a, e.

English 1.
1a, b, c. 2a, c, d.
3a, c.

Question 4 Do you think that Leroy and Linda were old enough and sensible enough to look after two guinea pigs?

Why did Leroy and Linda say they could not look after the guinea pigs? Were they too tired? Do you think they would be better able to look after a pet when they were older? Do you think they might be better able to keep their promises when they were older?

Question 5 Do all living things need to be cared for? How do people care for you?

PSHE
2a, e. 4d.

English I.
I a, c. 2a, c, d. 3a, c.

Do all living things need to be cared for? Do they need food, water and shelter? Who provides food, water and shelter for you? Are there other things that you do not need but want?

Question 6 Do you have a pet and how do you care for your pet?

What would be the promises you would make to your pet? Does everybody want the same kind of pet? Do all pets need the same sort of care? Does a goldfish need to go for a walk? Does a dog need to go for a walk? Does a cat need a hutch? Does a rabbit need a hutch?

PSHE
2a, e. 4c.

Supplementary ideas

Below are two lists – one with things which are alive, and one with things which are not alive:

Alive	Not alive
dogs	tables
cats	chairs
horses	computers
cows	robots
birds	hammers
fish	spoons
trees	pens
plants	toy cars
flowers	counting blocks.
rabbits.	

The teacher gathers the children onto the carpet. He selects an item from the above two lists, in random order, and asks the children if they are alive or not alive. Then he asks the children to put up their hands if they can think of anything which is alive or not alive. The children are then gathered into groups of four for an art lesson. Some groups have paint and brushes, other groups have modelling material, and some groups have collage material and glue. The task is to make two things, something that is alive and something that is not alive. Before the children begin the task the teacher discusses with the children what they are going to make. No two children in the same group should paint, or make a collage or model of the same items. The items can be mounted on a large frieze and displayed. Captions should be added. The teacher might select some of the following or think of other appropriate captions themselves.

PSHE
2e. 5f.

English 2.
1f.

Science 2.
1a.

'These things are alive.'
'These things are not alive.'
'These things need food, water and shelter.'
'These things do not need food and water."
'This plant needs, food, water and light to grow.'

Under each painted, collaged or modelled work the teacher could write the name of the item to help with the reading task.

The children are gathered onto the carpet. The teacher explains that we do some things for animals and that they do some things for us. The children are asked to put their hands on their heads if they think the animal is doing something for people and to cross their arms if they think people are doing something for the animal.

PSHE
2e.

English 1.
2a.

'I am a cat and I like it when I am given a tasty dinner.'
'I am a dog and I love it when I am taken out for a walk.'
'I am a guide dog for the blind and I take my human friend through the crowds and across the roads.'
'I am a rabbit and sometime people like to stroke me.'
'I am a guinea pig and I like it when my owner strokes me.'
'I am a hearing dog for the deaf and I tell my owner when the telephone rings.'
'I am a horse and I like to give people rides.'
'I am a goldfish and I like to swim in good water.'

The teacher gathers the children onto the carpet. He tells the children that he is going to read them some questions and they have to guess what the living thing is. He tells them to put up their hand when they think they know.

- I need a warm hutch.
  I have no tail.
  I need food and water and shelter.
  Leroy and Linda were too tired to look after me so Shama did.
  My initials are G. P.
  I am a _____ (guinea pig).

136

- I need food, water and shelter.
  I need big long walks in order to keep fit.
  I need a collar and lead in order to keep safe.
  I need a name tag if I get lost.
  I am a _____ (dog).

- I need fresh hay and a stable.
  I need food and water.
  I need to be shod with metal shoes.
  I like to take people for a ride.
  I usually wear a saddle when I take people for a ride.
  I am a _____ (horse)

- I have feathers.
  I need a nest to lay my eggs.
  I have wings in order to fly.
  I need food to be put out for me in winter and then I won't starve.
  I need water to drink and cannot cope with iced up water.
  I am a _____ (bird)

- I need light and water.
  I have a thick trunk to take food and water to my leaves.
  Sometimes people shelter under me when it is raining.
  I am a _____ (tree).

- You can spin my woolly coat into wool for jumpers and cardigans.
  I grow fresh wool for the winter.
  I live in fields in the summer.
  My young are called lambs.
  I am a _____ (sheep).

- I like to be stroked.
  I need to keep snug and warm so I like fires.
  I say meow.
  I am a _____ (cat).

The teacher can write and read some 'what am I' riddles of his own to the children.

The teacher gathers the children onto the carpet. He asks them what birds need us to do for them in winter in order to thrive and in some cases to stay alive. It is important to feed the birds and to keep their drinking water from freezing by breaking the ice and giving them fresh water. The teacher has a group of items which he displays in turn and asks what could be given to the birds either on a bird table, hanging from a tree or on the ground:

> Bread crumbs
> Tea bags
> Peanuts
> Sunflower seeds
> Pencil sharpenings
> Counting blocks
> Water
> Commercial bird seed
> An empty bottle which has contained medicine
> A teddy bear or other toy.

The children are encouraged by the teacher to feed the birds in winter at home and school.

The children sit at their desks. Each child makes a drawing of the animal they would most like to own. The children then come to the front of the class and display their work. They tell the class why they think that animal would make the best pet for them and why. The teacher may need to ask them questions to elicit the information. For example:

- What do you like best about this animal?

- Why is this pet better than another animal?

- Are there other things which are important about owning this pet?

- Is this pet good to stroke, feed, take for walks or ride?

- Is this important to you?

The teacher can contact the RSPCA and ask if someone is available to come and talk to the class about animal issues.

(The RSPCA will send or give information and advice about lesson planning, curriculum links and course development or provide inset courses. The RSPCA aims to promote kindness and prevent cruelty to animals. They provide a free magazine called Animal Focus, for primary school teachers. Website: www.rspca.org.uk

Worksheet instructions

"When you have a pet you have to promise the pet that you will look after it. Wild birds also need food in winter, and we can promise to make sure our bird table is always full. All animals need us to give them the right things (or conditions). All animals including birds and fish need shelter, food and drink and love. What promises do we make to our pets and other animals? Match and colour the pictures on your worksheet."

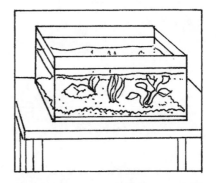

The Guinea Pigs

"I want a pet," said Linda.

"I want a pet," said Leroy.

"We want two pets," the twins chanted. "We want two guinea pigs."

Brenda, the twins' mum, thought the twins were too young to look after pets, and Josh, their dad, agreed.

He said, "No pets yet."

Leroy shouted, "I will look after my pet. I promise."

"And I will look after my pet too. I promise. I will, I will, I will," yelled Linda.

Every day Leroy and Linda asked for two guinea pigs.

"When can we have some pets?" they begged.

They pestered their mum and dad and would not stop.

They said, "Please, please, please," a million times.

"Please can we have two guinea pigs?"

In the end Brenda said that she would ask for Shama's advice.

Shama lent Brenda a book called *Caring for your Guinea Pigs*.

They had to have a warm, dry place to sleep and some fresh food and water each day. They also had to have a safe place in which to run about and play.

"I suppose I could make a hutch for the guinea pigs and I could make a run too," said Josh to his wife.

"And I could ask for the spare vegetable leaves from the kitchen in Morningdale Court," said Brenda. "They have fresh vegetables every day."

So after a lot of thinking Brenda and Josh told the twins that they could have two guinea pigs if they promised to look after them. "Every morning before you go to school you will have to give them some food and fresh water," said Josh. "You must promise."

"You must help me to clean out their hutch and give them some fresh straw for a nice warm bed," said their mum. "You must promise."

"We will, we will, we will," shouted Leroy and Linda together. "We promise, promise, promise."

And that is how Leroy and Linda got Joan and Jess.

The children were delighted. They made sure that Joan and Jess had some fresh food, water and straw each day. They helped to clean the hutch and they loved and cuddled the baby guinea pigs.

They said that they were the best guinea pigs in the whole world.

But bit-by-bit the twins grew tired of looking after Joan and Jess. They wanted all the fun of watching them and stroking them, but they didn't want to look after them.

"It makes me too tired at school if I have to get up early to feed the guinea pigs," said Linda.

"I will give the guinea pigs some water when I come home from school," said Leroy.

The twins started to complain about looking after their pets.

"Jenny can do it," said Leroy.

"Yes, Jenny likes pets," said Linda.

Josh and Brenda shouted at the twins.

"NO! you two must do the work. They are your pets, and you promised to look after them."

But Linda sulked and Leroy sulked and they both cried.

"We are too TIRED," they moaned.

"We are too tired to go out into the garden every morning. We have to work hard at school all day you know," the twins protested.

It was getting hard for Brenda and Josh too. They had to pull the twins out of bed each morning and make them go outside to look after their pets.

In the end Josh said he was putting up with the situation no longer and he asked Shama the student vet who lived next door if she would look after the guinea pigs.

Shama said she would, and that Joan and Jess could come and live with her guinea pigs. So Josh carried Joan and Jess into Shama's garden and put them in the run with her three guinea pigs called, Juliet, Helen and Katie.

When Leroy and Linda came home from school that day they went into their garden to play. They did not notice that Joan and Jess were not there.

When they came home from school the next day they went into their garden to play and again they did not notice that Joan and Jess were not there. They forgot all about their promise.

And the same thing happened the next day and the next day and the next.

It was five days before the twins noticed that Joan and Jess were not there.

"Where are Joan and Jess?" they cried.

Leroy shouted at Linda, "It's your fault, you promised to look after them."

Linda shouted at Leroy, "No, it's your fault, you promised to look after them."

They each blamed the other. They said that each other had broken their promise.

Leroy thought that Joan and Jess must have run away to find some food and they were sad because they didn't have a good home.

Linda cried, "I think that they are dead because they didn't have any food for days and days and days."

Leroy and Linda were both very upset.

They tried to blame Jenny.

"It's your fault if Joan and Jess have run away," said Linda.

"Yes, it's your fault if Joan and Jess are dead," said Leroy.

"You should have helped us, Jenny. You are our big sister, we are only little children," they said, and then they started to hit Jenny.

Josh was very angry with the twins. He had heard what they were saying to Jenny and he saw them hitting her.

Josh grabbed hold of Leroy with his right hand and he grabbed hold of Linda with his left hand. He stopped them hitting Jenny and he held the twins firmly in his grasp.

"You two wanted Joan and Jess and they were your pets. It was your responsibility to look after them. It is no use blaming Jenny, it was not her job; it was not her promise, but yours."

Then Josh told Leroy and Linda that he had had the baby guinea pigs adopted. He said that they were now in a home where they would be loved and cared for every day.

Leroy and Linda looked at their dad in disbelief.

"Yes," said Josh, "Joan and Jess are now being very well cared for and they have a good home, with Shama next door, and you can see them any-time you want to."

Leroy and Linda looked at Josh and they knew he was telling them the truth. "Little guinea pigs and all pets have to be looked after each day, just like little children," he told them gently and then asked them to think of what would happen to them if they didn't have anything to eat or drink for days. "What would happen if mum and I didn't keep our promise to look after you?"

"We would die," Leroy replied, and Linda said, "Yes, we would be dead."

That night when the children went to bed Brenda heard Leroy say to Linda,

"We were too young to have pets, Linda and we broke our promise."

"Yes," said Leroy, "I'm not going to have another pet until next year."

"Will you be old enough then, Leroy?" his sister asked.

"I don't know, Linda. "I will have to think first. Can I do it? Can I really look after pets every day? Can I keep my promise?"

"Yes," said Linda thoughtfully, "and I will have to tell you Leroy that you will have to look after your pets every day or else they will die and you will have to tell me that as well."

Lesson 13: February

Story: The Accident
Theme: Disaster and Recovery

Synopsis

Disaster strikes when baby Zoë gets a brazil nut stuck in her throat. Sali her mother runs for help and, regardless of her own safety, finds appropriate assistance in the guise of Dr Benson who recovers the situation most effectively. The story emphasises how Dr Benson keeps a cool head in an emergency.

Objectives

- To recognise what is fair and unfair and what is right and wrong.

- To share their opinions and to explain their views.

- To take part in discussion.

- To realise that other people have needs and that they have responsibilities to meet them.

- To learn that they belong to a neighbourhood.

- To know about people who can help them to stay safe.

- To recognise how their behaviour affects other.

- To know that friends should care for one another.

Preparing for the story

The teacher prepares a list of people who help us to stay safe and other people that do not or do help in an emergency. The children have to respond and say whether that person or thing helps us to stay safe and the teacher will put a cross or tick by its side.

> mum or dad
> a pet cat or dog
> ambulance people or paramedics
> a doctor or nurse

minibeasts
teachers
a lollipop person or school crossing person
a toy
a fire fighter
a kaleidoscope
a robot.

PSHE
3g.

Read the story

After the above activity has been completed the teacher reads the story to the children.

Circle Time discussion

PSHE
2a. 3g.

English 1.
1a, b, c. 2a, c, d.
3a, c.

Question 1 When baby Zoë got a brazil nut stuck in her throat did Tim do a sensible thing when he ran to get Dr. Benson?

Did Tim do the right thing when he said to the children "Get out of my way?" Had Tim gone to fetch someone who could help baby Zoë? What is an emergency? If Tim had asked Ronnie Calderbank to help would it have been as good as asking Dr. Benson to help? Why not?

Question 2 Baby Zoë got a brazil nut stuck in her throat when Sali was out of the room for a short while. Should babies be left unattended?

PSHE
2a. 3g.

English 1.
1a, b, c. 2a, c, d.
3a, c.

Should Sali have really watched baby Zoë all the time? Can grownup carers really watch their baby all the time? How could Sali have kept baby Zoë safe? Could she have carried baby Zoë in her arms when she went out to see what Tim was doing? Do grown-up people sometimes make mistakes?

PSHE
2a. 3g.

English 1.
1a, b, c. 2a, c. d.
3a, c.

Question 3 Why did Dr. Benson not rush over to Sali when she fell?

Was Dr. Benson's time taken up by helping baby Zoë? Was baby Zoë's need greater than Sali's? Could Dr. Benson do two things at once?

PSHE
2a, e, f. 4d.

English 1.
1a, b, c. 2a, c, d.
3a, c.

Question 4 Were Leroy, Linda and Paul sensible? How did they show they cared?

Do you think that Paul minded when Dr. Benson grabbed his sleigh? Was Linda kind when she lent Sali her scarf? Did Linda mind when her scarf was ruined? Did the children know that something was wrong?

Question 5 How did Sali show she cared for baby Zoë?

Did Sali think about her own safety when she rushed and fell in the snow or was she thinking of baby Zoë?

Question 6 Why did the ambulance come?

Did Dr. Benson call for an ambulance? Was it a sensible suggestion of Paul's that Sali and Zoë should go to hospital on his sleigh? Are ambulance people able to help us when we are hurt? If Sali had scratched herself would Dr. Benson have called an ambulance?

PSHE
2a. 4d.

English 1.
1a, b, c. 2a, c, d.
3a, c.

PSHE
2a. 3g.

Supplementary ideas

The children sit in a circle on the carpet and the teacher acts as scribe. The teacher has a large sheet of paper and on it is written:

'Our rules on how to keep safe in the snow and ice.'

The teacher asks the children if the following rules are silly or sensible. Why? She writes down the sensible rules under the heading of 'How to keep safe in the snow and ice'.

- Always tell a teacher if someone has been hurt on the snow and ice in the playground.

- Always tell your teddy bear if someone has been hurt on the snow and ice in the playground.

- Never drop litter in the snow and ice.

- Icy rivers are not dangerous.

- Banana skins should be dropped onto the snow and ice.

- Never, ever, skate on frozen ponds, rivers or lakes or other frozen water.

- Always take care not to slip on snow or ice.

- Always wear clothes to keep you warm in the snow and ice.

- Wear a swimming costume in the playground when it is snowy or icy.

- Never make slides on the pavement.

- Make slides where people can slip on them.

PSHE
1a. 3g. 4a.

(The teacher emphasises the consequences of the above actions and why some actions may be dangerous.)

The teacher gathers the children together on the carpet. She has a bag of various clothing and materials that are not suitable for a snowy day and clothes, and materials that are suitable for a snowy day. Which items would they choose for a snowy day?

PSHE
1b. 3a.

Science 3.
1a.

The children could get ready for an art lesson and make collages of woollen, velvet and other heavy materials, and also collages of cotton, silk, satin and other light materials which are suitable for a summer's day. The children could draw pictures of themselves on a snowy or icy day. The teacher asks them to draw (around the picture of themselves) items of footwear and clothing. She asks some volunteers to display their work to the class and to explain why they have chosen the clothes that they have drawn.

PSHE
3g.

The children gather on the carpet to talk about the dangers to be avoided on a snowy or icy day. The teacher could draw a picture of a road with vehicles travelling on it. What dangers are there on the roads on icy and snowy days? Should people drive quickly or slowly on a cold and icy or snowy day? Is putting sand and salt on the road a good idea? Why do we put sand and salt on the roads?

Worksheet instructions

"Here are some things which could be harmful to children and babies. Look at the worksheet. A circle has been put around the nails and screws to show that this is harmful. Can you tell me which other ones could be harmful."

(The teacher listens to the children's suggestions and helps them to identify the correct items.)

"Now circle the items which are harmful and colour in the picture."

The Accident

All the children in The Crescent were very happy because it had snowed. They were all playing on the big open space outside. Paul's dad had made a sleigh and Leroy and Linda had a large plastic dustbin lid to play with. It was an old dustbin lid and Josh, their dad, had fixed a rope to it. Leroy and Linda were using this as a sleigh. It was great fun.

Some of the other children had also come to play in The Crescent. They were all playing very happily together. They were laughing and shouting as they threw snowballs at each other.

"Here's Tim," shouted Paul. "Let's snowball him."

Paul had seen Tim. He was running from his house across the green. The children all began to snowball Tim. Leroy tried to push Tim over in the snow.

"Come and pull our sleigh, Tim," Linda shouted excitedly.

The children were very surprised when Tim shouted back at the children in a very angry way.

"Get out of my way," he yelled and rushed into Dr. Benson's surgery.

Within a few minutes both Tim and Dr. Benson were rushing back across the green. They were running to Number 1 The Crescent.

"Something must be wrong," said Paul very seriously, as he ran over the snow towards Tim's house. He was pulling his sleigh behind him. All his friends followed.

Then there was a big scream. It was Sali. She was holding baby Zoë in her arms.

"Oh! Please, please, come quickly," she was shouting as she ran towards Tim and Dr. Benson, Sali nearly threw baby Zoë into Dr. Benson's arms and as she did she slipped and fell on the slippery snow, and gave another big scream. Tim tried to pull Sali up and he tried to look at Dr. Benson at the same time. He was saying, "It's alright, Sali, calm down. Dr. Benson is looking after Zoë."

Sali stood up, her legs were shaking and her head was bleeding. There were red patches on the white snow.

All the children stood looking in amazement. They didn't know what was happening.

"Here, have my scarf for a bandage, Sali," said Linda as she pulled her scarf from around her neck and gave it to Sali.

"Dr. Benson, Dr. Benson," yelled Leroy, "Sali's bleeding, Sali's bleeding."

But Dr. Benson was taking no notice of Sali. He was grabbing hold of Paul's sleigh.

"Here, give me that sleigh," he shouted at Paul.

Dr. Benson sat down on the sleigh and holding baby Zoë in his arms he turned her upside down and gave her a big hit on her back.

Baby Zoë coughed and Dr. Benson hit her again on her back and as he did so baby Zoë coughed and choked even louder. Then she spluttered, gave another big cough and a Brazil nut landed in the snow just by Tim's feet.

Zoë cried, and then she smiled and then she cried again. Tim and Sali laughed too. They looked very happy except for all the blood on Sali's face.

We should get them both to the hospital," said Dr. Benson, who was now standing up and looking at Sali's head.

"I would like baby Zoë to have a hospital check-up, and Sali definitely needs some stitches in that nasty cut," he said. "What did you hit your head on, Sali? It must have been something sharp to give you a big cut like that."

"It was Tim's big snow boots," said Sali. "Tim was clearing the snow and I just came out to watch him for a minute and that is when Zoë must have found the Brazil nut and swallowed it. I couldn't get it out of her throat. It was stuck and poor Zoë was choking. I was so very worried and scared."

Sali unwrapped the scarf from her head. It was a white scarf and it looked very messy and blood stained.

"Oh dear," groaned Sali. "What a mess I have made of your scarf. I will buy you a new one, Linda."

But Linda said that it didn't matter and that she wanted Sali and baby Zoë to be better.

"Now, off you all go to hospital," said Dr. Benson in a firm voice, and he told Tim to go and ask nurse Emma to give him a big sterile bandage for Sali's head. "And tell her to call for an ambulance too."

Paul patted Dr. Benson on the arm and said very kindly,

"They can borrow my big sleigh to go to the hospital. I think Tim could pull Sali and baby Zoë to hospital. It's a big sleigh."

"You are all very kind children," said Dr. Benson. "It's my day off and I am not supposed to be working today. I think that we had better send them to hospital in an ambulance though."

Within a few minutes an ambulance pulled up outside Number 1 The Crescent, and Tim, Sali and baby Zoë got in.

All the children waved goodbye as the ambulance drove them off to hospital.

"I once choked on something when I was a baby," said Linda.

"Yes, she did," shouted Leroy being silly. "She once swallowed a worm."

"No, I didn't," Linda shrieked. "Leroy is telling lies."

"Yes, she did. She found it on a cabbage in the garden," Leroy shouted, being even sillier.

"Well, then Leroy choked on the cabbage," yelled Linda, because he tried to swallow the big cabbage."

Next Linda pushed Leroy, and the two children fell over in the snow laughing.

"Hey, you two, I don't want to deal with any more accidents today," Dr Benson shouted. "It's my day off, don't forget, and I want a ride on that sleigh."

All the children laughed as Dr. Benson sat down on the sleigh and Paul tried to pull the rope.

"Come and help me," shouted Paul. "But mind that red patch."

And very soon all the children were pulling Dr. Benson round and round in circles on Paul's sleigh in the snow.

Lesson 14: February

> **Story:** The Laugh
>
> **Theme:** Laughter and Derision

Synopsis

Baby Zoë laughs for the first time in response to a happening at a wedding. Laughter releases tension and all is well. The story deals with how laughter can transform a situation from the negative to the positive and can be of real communicative value between people.

Objectives

- To recognise what is fair and unfair.

- To take part in discussions.

- To understand that they belong to different communities including family.

- To understand that family and friends should care for one another.

- To feel positive about themselves.

Preparing for the story

The game 'Simon Says' is played using emotional expressions. The teacher explains to the children that if she starts the sentence with "Simon says", they must follow the action but if she says, "Make an expression," without saying "Simon says", then they have been caught out. (The teacher acts as a model in the first instance but she can use another model of her choice later in the game.) Examples of what to say follow:

"Simon says smile for the camera."
"Simon says look sad."
"Simon says look happy."
"Simon says look angry, frightened, shy, embarrassed, mad, delighted etc."
"Pull a funny face to make someone laugh."

PSHE
1c.

153

Read the story

After the above activity has been completed the teacher reads the story to the children.

Circle Time discussion

PSHE
2a. 4d.

English 1.
1a, b, c. 2a, c, d.
3a, c.

Question 1 At the beginning of the story Paul laughed - do you remember why?

Did he laugh because Paul said he would smuggle him in to Gemalli's wedding? Did Tim and Sali share in Paul's happiness? Did Tim and Sali care for Paul, their neighbour, as well as Zoë, their daughter? Was Paul glad that he was included in the wedding? Is it nice to get an invitation?

PSHE
1c. 2a.

English 1.
1a, b, c. 2a, c, d.
3a, c.

Question 2 Are people often happy and smiling at a wedding and do photographs of weddings often show happy people?

Do you ever look at wedding photographs? Is a wedding a celebration? What is being celebrated? Do people often smile and laugh at a celebration? Have you ever been to other celebrations? What were they? (Birthdays, anniversaries, festivals, carnivals etc.) Were the people who went to the celebrations happy? Did they smile or laugh?

PSHE
1c. 2a.

English 1.
1a, b, c. 2a, c. d.
3a, c.

Question 3 Did everyone in the story laugh together?

Can you remember a time when you laughed and did you laugh with other people? Is it nice to laugh with other people? Do you laugh more if other people are laughing? Is it good to tell jokes?

PSHE
1c. 2a.

English 1.
1a, b, c. 2a, c, d.
3a, c.

Question 4 Is it always kind to laugh?

Has anybody ever laughed at you and you didn't like it? Is it kind to laugh because someone has fallen or made a mistake? When Tim fell in the pond did he think it was funny right away?

Question 5 Was Zoë a happy baby girl?

Did Zoë smile a lot? Did this show that she was happy? Did Zoë laugh? Is there a difference between laughing and smiling? Do both things show that you are happy or sad?

PSHE
1c. 2a.

English 1.
1a, b, c. 2a, c, d.
3a, c.

Question 6 Who or what makes you laugh?

Who on television makes you laugh? Do cartoons make you laugh? Do clowns make you laugh? Why do they make you laugh? Do any books make you laugh?

PSHE
1c. 2a.

English 1.
1a, b, c. 2a, c, d.
3a, c.

Supplementary ideas

The teacher brings in pictures and photographs of various celebrations, for example weddings, carnivals, festivals or birthdays. Can the children guess what the people in the picture or photograph are celebrating? Are some of the people laughing or smiling? Can the children tell of celebrations or festivals where they have been? Can they tell what they liked and disliked?

PSHE
1a. 2f.

The story of Zoe's first laugh is about the taking of photographs. The teacher or adult helper takes photographs of the children in groups or at play. (Make sure that you have at least one photograph for each child). The teacher or adult helper makes up a photograph album with simple captions, for example:

'John, Helen and Juliet are playing tag in the playground.' 'They are enjoying themselves.'

'Nadif and Susan are dressed as a prince and princess in the dressing up corner. Don't they look good?'

'Martin, Sali and Katie are dressed in their PE kit. They like PE.'

PSHE
5b.

'Here are Truda, Kenneth and Tom making good models with clay.'

Children get into groups of four. Two children pose as if at a wedding. Are they smiling for the camera? The other two children draw or colour their faces only. Remember to include their expression.

PSHE
1c.

The teacher discusses with the children how Sali felt when the photographer tried to be in two places at the same. The photographer was late for the wedding. Is it important to be punctual and on time?

PSHE
1a, c. 3a.

Was it fair or unfair of the photographer? How did it make others feel? Did Sali feel sad?

The teacher tells the children that they are going to play 'shadows' with emotional expressions. The children go into the hall and find a partner. They must decide who is going to be the 'leader' first and who is going to be follower. The children stand face to face. The leader makes an emotional expression of sadness, happiness, anger etc.; the follower makes the same expression. The leader and follower then change roles and repeat the process.

Worksheet instructions

"Look at your worksheet. You will find a television screen. Draw somebody or something which makes you laugh on the television screen."

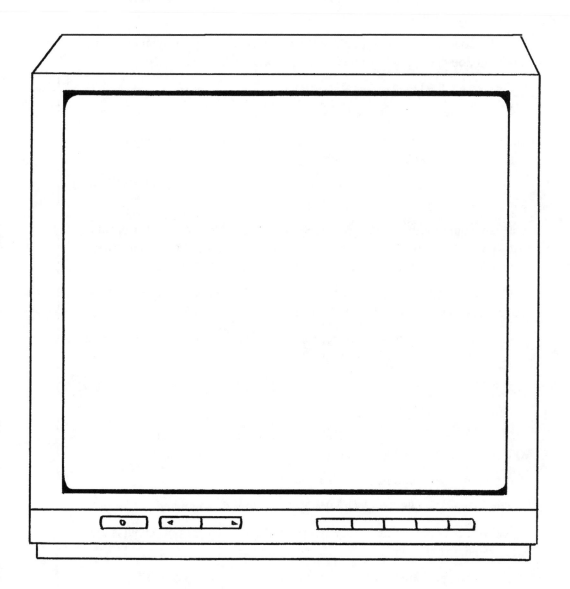

Lesson 14

The Laugh

Sali was wondering why her baby Zoë never laughed. Zoë smiled all the time. She was a happy baby but she never laughed.

Sali tried to make her laugh and Tim tried to make her laugh. He pulled funny faces but Zoë did not laugh. She just smiled and smiled and smiled.

"Why doesn't Zoë laugh?" Sali asked Tim.

Tim just shook his head. He didn't know, and Zoë smiled at him.

Tim went out into the garden to plant some flowers. Paul came along with his truck and asked Tim if he could help.

"Sure you can," said Tim. He handed Paul a small trowel and asked him to dig a small hole for the plant he was holding.

Sali came out into the garden. She was carrying Zoë. Zoë smiled at Paul, who was now enjoying watering the plant that Tim had put into the ground. Then Paul looked round. The postman was coming to No. 1 The Crescent.

Paul always liked it when the postman arrived. The postman handed the letters to Paul and Paul handed the letters to Sali.

"This looks a very interesting envelope," she said as she looked at one of their letters. The envelope was decorated with roses.

"Let's go inside the house and see who it's from," said Tim.

So they all went indoors. They invited Paul in too.

"It's a wedding invitation," said Sali in a very happy voice. "It's from Gemalli, Oh! Tim, how lovely, Gemalli was my bridesmaid at our wedding."

Zoë smiled at her mummy as if she knew that Sali was happy.

"I don't know Gemalli," said Paul. He looked rather disappointed.

"Well, you can come to the wedding if you wish to," said Sali. "Gemalli is my best friend. I shall tell her that you are coming."

"I shall smuggle you in," said Tim, giving Paul a big hug as he spoke.

Paul laughed at that idea. He thought it sounded good fun.

Zoë gave a huge smile. She was watching Paul.

"Would you like to see a picture of Gemalli when she was a bridesmaid at our wedding?" Sali asked Paul. Paul said that he would like that. So it wasn't long before they were all looking at the wedding photograph album.

Zoë looked too. She liked picture books and she seemed to recognise mummy and daddy in the photographs because she smiled.

There were two sets of photographs. The professional photographer took one set and Tim took the other set.

"Why did you take photographs on your own wedding day?" Paul asked Tim.

"Because," answered Tim, "the silly man went to the wrong church which was miles away and he didn't arrive until the reception was almost over. So I had to be photographer at my very own wedding!"

Paul laughed at that and Zoë smiled and smiled.

"Tell Paul about the funny thing you did when you were taking photographs, Tim," said Sali.

"Well," said Tim looking directly at Paul, "Sali was so upset because the photographer was not at our wedding that she almost cried. I tried to make jokes about it but that didn't work."

"I tried to tickle Sali but that made her even more upset. We all tried everything we could think of but Sali would not smile. I said that I would be photographer and I asked my best man to lend me his camera."

"Smile please," I shouted to Sali and I stepped back to get a clearer picture of her. But what I didn't realise was that there was a goldfish pond immediately behind me. We were all in the grounds of the hotel where our reception was being held at the time."

"Then, 'Splash'! I stepped right back into the goldfish pond and guess what? Yes, Sali laughed. She laughed and laughed and laughed."

"At that very moment our real photographer turned up. He was just in time to get a picture of me with socks, shoes and trousers all wet."

Then Tim handed Paul the photograph of himself with his trousers all soaking wet and lots of pond weed stuck to his shoes.

Paul thought it was a hilarious story and a very funny picture and he started to laugh. Sali got the giggles again and she couldn't stop laughing.

Tim said, "I didn't think it was very funny at the time." But then he laughed too.

Then, what do you think happened next? I suppose you have guessed. Yes, baby Zoë laughed and laughed and laughed.

Then they were all laughing at Zoë's laughter.

"Zoë has laughed for the very first time," said Tim.

"Yes," said Sali, "she knows a funny story when she hears one."

Lesson 15: March

> **Story:** **The Wedding**
> **Theme: Weddings and Formalities**

Synopsis

Mum is adamant that Leroy and Linda must dress appropriately for a wedding even if they would prefer to 'dress up'. The story deals with the correct code of conduct for a formal situation.

Objectives

● To recognise what is fair and unfair and what is right and wrong.

● To recognise, name and deal with their feelings.

● To realise that money comes from various sources.

● To know that family and friends should care for each other.

Preparing for the story

The teacher gathers the children around her on the carpet. She has various kinds of clothing in a large box. The children have to say who might wear them and when they might be worn. Items that might be included are:

a bridesmaid's dress
wellington boots
dance shoes
ballet slippers
PE kit
bow tie
any dress from other cultures
clothes from the dressing up box.

What clothes would they choose for a PE lesson or a wedding? Would it be wrong to choose a bow tie for a swimming lesson?

PSHE
2a, c.

Read the story

After the above activity has been completed the teacher reads the story to the children.

Circle Time discussion

PSHE
1a. 2a, f. 4d.

English 1.
1a, b, c. 2a, c, d. 3a, c.

Question 1 Have you ever been to a wedding?

What is a wedding? When did you go to a wedding? Where did you go for the wedding? Are weddings special? Do family, friends and neighbours go to a wedding? Were the neighbours and friends of Matti and Ronnie going to a wedding? Did Leroy and Linda know the difference between a wedding and a party?

PSHE
1a. 2a.

English 1.
1a, b, c. 2a, c, d. 3a, c.

Question 2 Was it fair of Leroy and Linda to wear dressing up clothes for Ronnie's wedding?

Do you think that anyone else at Ronnie's wedding would be wearing dressing up clothes? Would it be right or wrong to wear dressing up clothes at Ronnie's wedding?

PSHE
1a. 2a.

English 1.
1a, b, c. 2a, c. d. 3a, c.

Question 3 Was Brenda, Leroy and Linda's mummy right to be cross with them?

Did Leroy and Linda dress as they were told? Should they have dressed as they were told? Had they disobeyed their mummy? Was this right or wrong?

PSHE
2a, f.

English 1.
1a, b, c. 2a, c, d. 3a, c.

Question 4 Why did Leroy and Linda change their minds and want to wear smart new clothes for Ronnie's wedding like the rest of their family?

Did Linda and Leroy think that everyone else looked smart in their new clothes? Did they want to look like everyone else in their family?

PSHE
2a, i.

English 1.
1a, b, c. 2a, c, d. 3a, c.

Question 5 On what occasions do you have to wear special clothes? Do clothes cost money? Who buys you your special clothes?

Does your school have a uniform? Do you wear special clothes for PE or swimming? Do you wear special clothes for parties? Do you wear special clothes when you go to bed? Do mum, dad and other relatives buy you clothes? Do you get clothes for presents?

Question 6 Families and friends get together at weddings. Do they get together at any other time?

PSHE
1c. 2a, f.

Do family and friends get together at birthdays, Christmas, or other religious festivals? Do they get together for holidays, feasts, barbecues and christenings? Do you think that other people might be happy at these times? Does it make you happy?

English 1.
1a, b, c. 2a, c, d. 3a, c.

Supplementary ideas

The teacher gives the children a piece of A4 drawing paper divided into four equal parts lengthways. The teacher tells them that they are going to draw themselves:

1. At a party.

2. Playing at tag with their friends in the playground.

3. When they are not feeling very well.

PSHE
1c.

4. Going to the shops on a rainy day.

How are they feeling? Give themselves an expression of happiness or sadness. What are they wearing? Think carefully about these two things, and put them in your drawings.

Art & Design
1a.

The children are gathered on the carpet. The teacher reads the following sentences to the children. The sentences are jumbled up and written on large strips of paper and the children's task is to say the correct order. The teacher tells them that the words, 'firstly', 'next' and 'finally' are a clue to the correct order.

> 'Next they got dressed in their wedding clothes.'
> 'Firstly Leroy and Linda got dressed.'
> 'Finally they went to Ronnie's wedding.'

English 2.
1i.

The teacher tells the children that she is going to read some rules for formal occasions. If the rule is silly the children should put their fingers on their nose. If it is sensible they must fold their arms.

> 'Always wear a Mickey Mouse outfit.'
> 'Wear flowers on your clothes or in your hair.'
> 'Wear a nice suit or dress.'
> 'Wear your swimming costume.'
> 'Always wear wellington boots.'
> 'Run and shout when you want to.'

PSHE
2c.

The teacher tells the children they are going to pretend that their parents or carer have got twenty pounds to buy a wedding present. Which items in the list could they buy? The children are told to put up their hands if they think the twenty pounds would be enough to pay for:

a new car
a television set
some drinking glasses
a vase
a plant and plant pot
a house.

PSHE
Ii.

Would a lot of different people buy wedding presents? What else do the children think they could buy for twenty pounds as a wedding present?

Worksheet instructions

"On your worksheet you will find an outline picture of a grown-up person and a child, they are going to a wedding. Dress the adult and child in suitable clothes to go to Ronnie and Matti's wedding.

Are they wearing shoes and a hat? Are they carrying anything? Perhaps they are carrying presents or a bag; perhaps they are carrying flowers. What are they wearing? Are they male (man or boy) or female (a woman or girl)? Are they wearing suits or dresses? Are they wearing ties or buttonholes? Do they have flowers in their hair?"

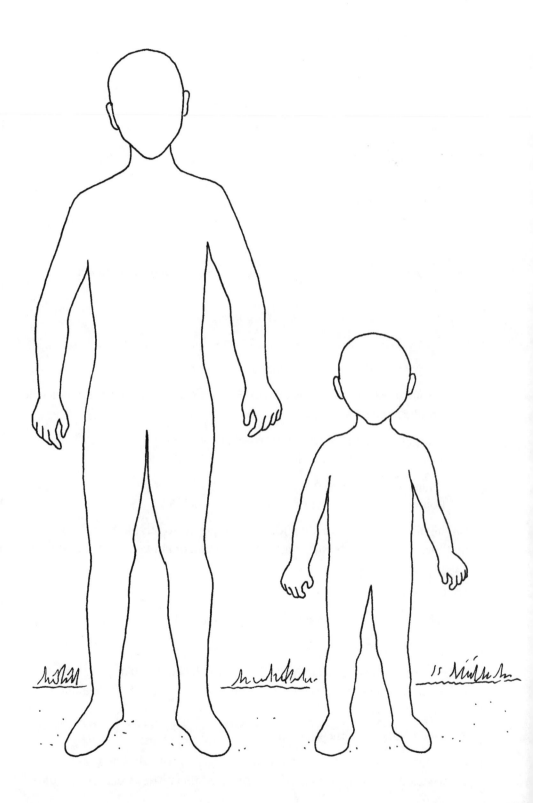

The Wedding

"We're going to a party," said Leroy to Ronnie.

"Yes, we're going to a party," said Linda. She was copying Leroy.

"You are going to a party too, Ronnie," said Leroy. "Matti is going to be there as well."

"You are not going to a party. You are going to a wedding, and it's my wedding," Ronnie told them.

"And Matti's wedding," said Linda.

Ronnie laughed. "Yes, Matti will have to be there, I hope she remembers to come."

"Will you be getting dressed up?" asked Linda.

"I certainly shall," Ronnie answered. "Matti will be dressing up as well."

"We are going to dress up in our fancy dressing-up clothes," Leroy announced.

"Yes, I think I will wear my cowboy clothes, or my pirate's costume. Linda will probably be a fairy," said Leroy.

"No, I won't. I won't be a fairy. That would be silly for a wedding. I will be a farmer, and then I can bring all my farm animals with me," Linda told them.

"Well, I am sure you will both look very smart whatever you come dressed up in," Ronnie smiled at the twins.

On the morning of the wedding Josh told the twins to put on the new clothes that their mother had bought for them. She had bought Leroy a smart shirt and a new pair of trousers.

Linda had a lovely new dress.

"I am not wearing those things," said Leroy indignantly.

"I am not wearing that dress," protested Linda.

"Oh! Please yourselves," said Josh. He couldn't be bothered arguing with the twins. He was waiting to go into the bathroom for a shower. Brenda and Jenny were getting ready too.

They were putting on their best clothes.

Meanwhile, Linda and Leroy had rushed off to find their dressing-up box. Linda was trying on a pair of yellow striped pyjamas. They were Jenny's old ones. Leroy was putting his face paints on. He was already wearing his pirate's clothes.

"Where are the twins, Jenny?" asked their mother.

"We're here, we're here," shouted Leroy and Linda. They came running and jumping out of their bedroom. They were very happy.

Their mother looked at them in disbelief.

"What do you think you are doing?" she scolded. "You are not going to a wedding like that. Whatever will Ronnie and Matti think if they see you in those silly clothes? Get changed immediately. You will make us late for the wedding."

"Daddy said we could please ourselves. He said we could get dressed up," Linda shouted at her mummy. "Ronnie knows we are coming in our dressing-up clothes. We told him and he said it would be alright."

"Yes, Ronnie said he thinks we will both look very smart," added Leroy.

Brenda was furious.

"You must go dressed appropriately. You must show some respect and you must look dignified. Get out of those clothes this very minute."

Leroy wailed, "It's not fair. I don't like my shirt and you are using big words."

Linda stamped and shouted, "I won't, I won't put on that silly new dress."

Josh came downstairs. He was wearing his new suit. He looked very smart.

Jenny came downstairs. She was dressed in her bridesmaid clothes. Ronnie and Matti had asked her to be a bridesmaid. She looked lovely.

Linda and Leroy looked at Jenny. Then they looked at Josh. They could see how good they looked in their new clothes. Josh had a carnation in his buttonhole. Jenny had flowers in her hair band. Brenda, their mum, was wearing a beautiful skirt and jacket. She had a spray of flowers pinned to her jacket.

The twins looked at themselves in the long mirror. They didn't look as if they were going to a wedding. They looked as if they were going to a dressing-up party.

"I want to wear my new clothes," said Leroy.

"I want to wear my new clothes," said Linda.

"I think you should go dressed as you are," said Josh.

"No! No! No!" shouted the twins. "We are going to a wedding not a dressing-up party."

Lesson 16: March

> **Story:** **The Surprise**
> **Theme:** **Birth and New Arrivals**

Synopsis

Linda is upset when she finds that her teacher is going to leave school for a while to have a new baby, but she accepts the inevitable and grows to like her new supply teacher (who is a man). She is surprised when he tells her he is expecting a baby too - he is going to be a daddy! A quiet introduction into the issues of birth and the father's role in the raising of a family.

Objectives

- To recognise what is fair and unfair.

- To think about themselves.

- To take part in discussion.

- To know that they belong to various groups and communities such as family and school.

- To realise that babies have needs.

- To realise that an individual grows older.

- To identify and respect differences between babies and older children and people.

- To meet and talk with people.

Preparing for the story

The teacher brings in a doll dressed in joggers and a top. She also brings in some cotton wool balls and some water in a dish, some food and some milk in a bottle, a hairbrush, socks and a hat and coat that fit the 'baby'. The teacher brings in a cot or cradle to fit the baby. She explains to the class that the doll is going to act as a model of a baby. The teacher explains that a doll is only a toy and does not have needs, but a real baby has real needs. The teacher shows the children the items of clothing and other items that she

169

has brought in to class. She will discuss with the children, an item at a time, what is the use of the item. The teacher or other adult will write down on the blackboard, whiteboard or large display what she has used and what need it fulfils.

Firstly the teacher shows the children the water and the cotton wool ball and washes the baby's hands and face.

The teacher shows the hairbrush and asks the children to put up their hands if they know what to do with the hairbrush. The child who has answered correctly comes out to the front and brushes the baby's hair.

The teacher shows the food and milk and asks the children to put up their hands if they know what should be done with the food and drink. The child who has answered correctly comes out to the front and mimes the action with empty food and milk containers.

The teacher shows the children the socks, hat and coat. She asks the children to put up their hands if they know what to do. The child who has answered correctly comes and puts the socks, hat and coat on the baby, (being encouraged to do this gently).

PSHE
2e.

The teacher explains that the baby is now tired. She asks the children what should happen next. (Put the baby in the cot, cradle or pram to sleep.) The child who has the right answer comes and puts the baby in the cradle. (They should be encouraged to rock the baby if that is possible.)

Read the story

After the above activity has been completed the teacher reads the story to the children.

Circle Time discussion

PSHE
1a. 2a.

English 1.
1a, b, c. 2a, c, d.
3a, c.

Question 1 Did Linda like or dislike the fact that her teacher was leaving to have a baby? Was it right or wrong, fair or unfair?

Are some teachers mummies or daddies as well as being teachers? Was Linda cross and jealous in the story? Why? Did Linda like her teacher? Did she also like the man supply teacher?

Question 2 Do you think Linda's teacher was special to her? Who else was special to Linda?

Were members of her family and neighbours special to Linda? Who is special to you?

PSHE
2a. f.

English I.
1a, b, c. 2a, c, d. 3a, c.

Question 3 Did Leroy and Linda think it was special to announce nice things to the class?

Is it nice to have a special job? What special jobs do you have at home or school? What are you good at?

PSHE
1d. 2a.

English I.
1a, b, c. 2a, c. d. 3a, c.

Question 4 What did Mr Fitzpatrick tell Leroy?

Do you think that Mr Fitzpatrick was excited that he was going to be a daddy? What do you think the baby would like him to do for him or her? Would the baby need a lot of care? What sort?

PSHE
2a, e.

English I.
1a, b, c. 2a, c, d. 3a, c.

Question 5 When the babies were born would they have needs and who would help to give them what they needed?

Would they need food and drink, shelter, warmth, love, play and sleep? Would they need anything else? Do mums and dad, brothers and sisters all help when there is a new baby to look after? Is this right and fair? What could you do to help a new baby?

PSHE
1a. 2a, e.

English I.
1a, b, c. 2a, c, d. 3a, c.

Question 6 Do we sometimes have new teachers?

When do we have a new teacher and why do we have a new teacher? Is it sometimes hard to get used to a new teacher? Did Leroy and Linda like their new teacher? How do you know? What things do you like and dislike?

PSHE
1a. 2a.

English I.
1a, b, c. 2a, c, d. 3a, c.

Supplementary ideas

PSHE
5e.

Invite in some parents to give a talk to the children about what their children need and what is good about being a mum or dad.

PSHE
2a, e. 4c.

English 1.
1a, b, c. 3a, c, d.
3a, c.

English 3.
4b, d, e.

Are the things that a baby needs, the same as things that everybody needs, or are they different? Make a display of the things that a baby needs. (The artefacts used for 'Preparing for the story' could be used). The children go into groups of four and are given paper, pencils and crayons. The teacher discusses with the children what a baby needs. Then the children draw what a baby needs. The children who are able to do so could label their drawings, some might be able to put a first letter on their drawing (e.g. 'B' for bottle) and should be encouraged to do so, some may copy from a model provided by the teacher, adult helper or older child.

Gather the children on the carpet. The teacher has a group of statements written on cards. She makes two spaces where cards may be put marked 'true' or 'untrue'. The statements are as follows:

PSHE
2e. 3d.

Science 2.
1b.

A baby is a living thing.
Newborn babies need milk.
Newborn babies like fish and chips.
I like fish and chips.
Babies grow up.
Dogs have puppies and human beings have babies.
One day I will be in the junior school.
Babies see with their teeth.

We use our nose to smell and our eyes to see the world around us.

Worksheet instructions

"The woman teacher, in the story, writes a letter to the class. This is what she says:

'My baby has been born and is well and healthy. The baby is six weeks old and is starting to smile. Lots of love to you all. From Mrs Dickinson.'

Now look at the top of your worksheet. There are some pictures of the cards that Mr Allsorts had in his shop. Now you draw and colour the card which you would have sent to the new baby."

The Surprise

"Our teacher is going to have a baby," Leroy said to Linda.

Linda looked surprised.

"No, she's not," said Linda. "You are being silly again, Leroy."

"Yes, she is. I know because I heard her talking to Mr. Manini, our headteacher, about a baby."

"Well, not her baby, though," Linda answered.

"Yes, it is her baby. Mr. Manini said he would lend her a car seat that they no longer needed. He said that his son Luigi was too big for a car seat now. I heard him say that."

"You are telling lies, Leroy. Our teacher can't have a baby. She is our teacher so she can't have a baby."

"Teachers can have babies, Linda. I know they can. Grown-up women can have babies if they want to."

"I know that," said Linda, "but not if they are at school teaching children like us."

"Then they just stop being teachers and go and get the baby born," Leroy told her.

"Our teacher can't have one," Linda shouted. "What will happen to us if she goes away and has a baby. We will be all on our own. Our teacher won't leave us all on our own. I don't like you, Leroy, for telling me that."

But it was true. Leroy was right. The next day in class their teacher told them that she was going to have a baby and that she would be leaving school before the end of the term.

Some children shouted, "Hooray!" Some children laughed. Some children asked her who the daddy was. Linda shouted out. "That's not fair." She ran out of the classroom and would not talk to her teacher all day. Linda was very cross.

"Why are you looking so cross?" Josh asked Linda, when he came to school to meet the twins at home time.

"It is because I was right," Leroy answered for her. "I told her that our teacher was going to have a baby and I am right and Linda is wrong."

"It's our teacher that is wrong. She is a very naughty teacher. I don't like her any more," snapped Linda.

The next day Linda wouldn't do any work for her teacher. Then the next day and the next it was the same. When her teacher tried to comfort her Linda told her to go away.

Soon everybody began to worry about Linda. They did not know what to do.

Her mummy told her not to worry.

Her daddy told her not to worry.

Jenny told her not to worry.

Even Leroy told her not to worry.

"We will get another teacher," Leroy told her, "and then it will be alright."

A few weeks later their teacher did leave. She gave all the children in her class a present before she left. She said that after the baby was born she would bring it to school to show it to them all.

A supply teacher arrived. Linda liked him and got on with her work very well.

His name was Mr Fitzpatrick. "You won't leave us like that horrid woman did, will you?" Linda asked.

Leroy laughed at Linda when he heard her say that.

"He won't leave us to go and have a baby, silly. He's a man." Leroy pushed Linda and ran away.

"Now I don't like boys," Linda told her friend Rosie.

After that Linda wouldn't talk to any boys in her class. Mr Fitzpatrick was rather worried about Linda. He didn't know what to do.

Then one day he heard the good news. The baby had arrived and it was a little girl.

"I want you to make an announcement in class today," said Mr. Fitzpatrick to Linda.

"I want you to say that the baby has arrived and that it is a girl. Her name is Emma Jane."

Linda felt very proud to be the one that had been told the good news first.

She made the announcement very well. She said that they should all make a card to send to the new baby. And they did.

"I was the one who first told you about our teacher's baby," said Leroy. "I think that I should be chosen to make the announcement."

"No, you shouldn't, Leroy," said Linda. "It should have been me because I am a girl. You are silly, Leroy."

"I'm going to tell Mr. Fitzpatrick about you," said Leroy. He was very angry with his sister.

So the next day Leroy told Mr. Fitzpatrick all about his difficult sister.

"Shall I tell you a secret, Leroy?" said Mr. Fitzpatrick. "You mustn't tell anybody else just yet, but I am going to be a daddy soon."

Leroy was very happy to be the one to be told the good news first.

"Is it alright if I just tell Linda and nobody else?" Leroy asked.

Mr. Fitzpatrick said, "Yes, that will be alright."

So that night Leroy said to Linda, "Our teacher is going to have a baby."

"Our teacher has had a baby already, Leroy. Don't forget I am the one who was chosen to make the announcement."

"No, I mean Mr. Fitzpatrick is going to have a baby."

"Don't be silly, Leroy," laughed Linda. "Teachers can't have babies. Well not if they are men."

"I know all about teachers and babies," said Leroy proudly.

And much to her surprise, Linda soon found out that Leroy was right.

Lesson 17: April

> **Story:**   **The Goose**
> **Theme:**   **Bullying and Friendship**

Synopsis

Sophie, who is blind, tells Leroy and Linda and Paul a story about a bullying gosling, Gregory, and how he is bullied in turn by Sylvia, a protective mother swan. The hapless Greg, bullied by Sylvia, flees, but after many adventures Greg is found by the repentant swan and mutual apologies occur. Finally Greg is welcomed home by all the birds. This story deal with the issue of bullying and how successful integration is made possible.

Objectives

- To understand what is right and wrong.

- To take part in a discussion.

- To recognise how their behaviour affects other people.

- To understand that family and friends should care for one another.

- To know that there are different kinds of teasing and bullying, that bullying is wrong and how to get help with bullying.

- To consider social and moral behaviour that they come across in everyday life.

Preparing for the story

The children sit round in a circle. They are asked to make up a pleasant name for themselves using the same initial as their name (for example, Lovely Leah, Gorgeous Gita, Sunshine Suzie, Beautiful Beverley, Bold Bertie, Amazing Ahmed). For young children the teacher could go through the alphabet first with suggestions (i.e. angelic, amazing, awesome, amiable). The children are asked to think of names which they would like to be called and names which they would not like to be called. The children are asked to put up their hand if they would like to say what these names are. They can be asked if they have got a nickname, and if so do they like or dislike their nickname? Are there times when name-calling hurts them and makes them sad or angry? Are there times when a nice name makes them happy and pleased?

Read the story

After the above activity has been completed the teacher reads the story to the children.

Circle Time discussion

Question 1 Were there some things that Gregory did that were wrong, unfair and disliked by other birds?

Did Greg splash the other ducks with water? Did he dive into the middle of the other ducks and take their food just for fun and not because he was hungry? Did he scare the little cygnets who were just starting to swim?

Question 2 Why did Greg start bullying?

Was he told to go and swim 'over there' because he was getting in the way? Was he the same as the other goslings in his family or was he bigger? Did he take any notice of his mother when she told him to stop bullying? Did he have to sleep alone, without the company of his brothers and sisters? How do you think Greg felt about this?

Question 3 Was there more than one bully in the story?

Was Paul bullying when he said that only Ronnie could play with him and not Leroy and Linda? Was Greg a bully when he splashed the other goslings and cygnets and took food from them? Did Sylvia bully Greg when she chased him away?

Question 4 Are bullies always the same people or can anyone be a bully? Do bullies look bad and evil or do they look just like you and me?

Can someone be bullied by someone and then bully someone else? Can bullies look big or small or smiley or frowny? Can bullies be friends sometimes and bullies other times? Can you sometimes be a bully? Why or why not?

Question 5 Who came searching for Gregory, found him and freed him?

A 'search party' is when someone goes searching for something or someone who is lost. Did Sylvia find Greg and free him? Should families care for one another? How did she free him? Were the man and his wife kind to Greg? Do you think that Greg was pleased to escape and go to the other birds on the river?

PSHE
2a. 4d, e.

English I.
I a, b, c. 2a, c, d.
3a, c.

Question 6 Was it nice for Greg to be given a welcome home party?

Did Sylvia and the other birds want to include Greg? How do you think Greg felt when he was included? Is there a connection between Greg being included and becoming 'the friendliest goose that ever lived'? Would you have given Greg a welcome home party? Did the story have a happy ending?

PSHE
2a. 4a, d.

English I.
I a, b, c. 2a, c, d.
3a, c.

Supplementary ideas

The teacher and children brainstorm things that you could say to a bully. Could you say 'no' to a bully; 'don't do that'; 'forget it'; 'stop kicking'; 'watch it'; 'must dash'? Is it better to deal with a bully yourself or tell other people like parents, teachers or dinner ladies? Would it be possible to do both?

PSHE
2a. 4e.

The teacher explains to the children that there was more than one bully in the story. Gregory bullied and Sylvia bullied. Paul said he didn't want to play with the twins or share his game so he was a bit of a bully. All of the bullies later wanted to make things better for their friends. Which of these things could make things better for your friends?

Share your pencils and crayons.
Shout, "Go away you can't play."
Smack your friends.
Let your friend play with you.
Push past your friend.
Nip or kick your friend.
Help your friend with their work if they are stuck.
Look at a book with your friend.
Read with your friend.
Play a game with your friend.
Call your friend nasty names.
Trip your friend up in the playground.

PSHE
4e.

Children get dressed for PE. The teacher arranges the children into pairs. The children each have a bean bag. The game is to throw it so their partner can catch the ball. The teacher and other adult helpers praise the children when they throw and catch making it easy for each other.

Worksheet instructions

"Can you see Gregory in the picture? He is bigger than the cygnets. He is trying to splash the cygnets but the cygnets are telling him not to be a bully. What are the cygnets saying to Gregory? Put up your hand to tell me what you think they are saying. I am going to write some things, which would be a good idea for the cygnets to say to Gregory, in the speech bubble. For example, 'Go away, don't splash here,' or 'Stop it at once'.

Now you copy the words in the speech bubble onto your picture. When you have finished the speech bubbles colour in your picture."

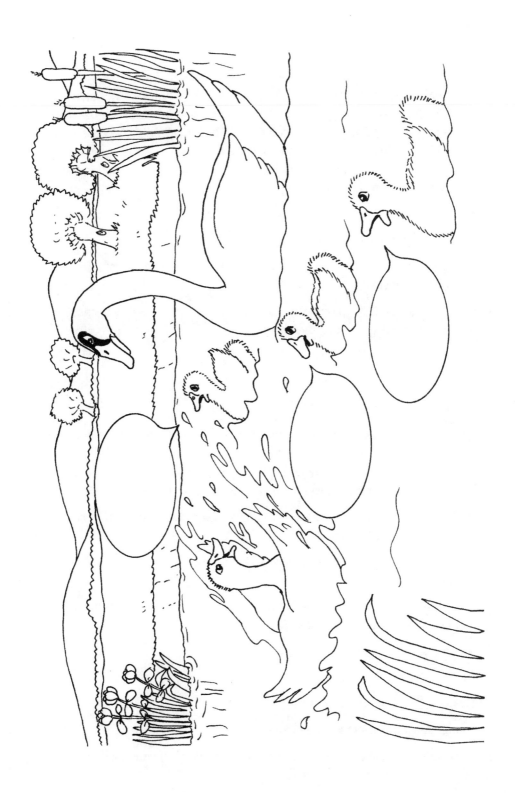

The Goose

The children in The Crescent were bored. The school holidays were almost over. The twins were quarrelling and Paul didn't want to play with them. He didn't want his friend Max to come to his house anymore because Max talked to Duncan and Duncan was a bit of a bully. Brenda was going over to Morningdale Court to help with the lunch-time meal. She was taking the twins with her. "Paul can come too," she said.

"I'm going to take my best game and ask Ronnie to play with me," said Paul.

"Can we play too?" asked the twins.

"No, you can't. You won't understand the rules and you will spoil it," replied Paul rather selfishly.

"Well," said Brenda, "No one can ask Ronnie for anything today because he is not there. He has gone on a day trip."

"That's not fair," said Leroy.

"No, it's not," said Linda, and stamped her foot.

Paul sulked and said, "Well, I'll do nothing then."

By this time Brenda was feeling rather fed up too. It was a dull day and it was raining now. When they arrived at Morningdale Court Hope came up to greet them. She gave them all a friendly lick and wagged her tail. She liked the children. The children followed Hope as she went back to sit at Sophie's side.

"Hello" said Sophie, "I'm glad that you have come. I haven't seen or spoken to anyone today. Ronnie is away."

Then she asked them how they were and she soon realised that they were feeling quarrelsome.

Paul told her about Max and how Max didn't mind playing with Duncan and that Duncan was a bit of a bully.

"I know a bully," said Linda.

"No you don't," said Leroy.

"Yes I do," replied Linda, "but he doesn't go to our school."

Sophie pulled Hope closer to her side.

"I sometimes make up stories," Sophie said. "Shall I tell you one?"

182

The children settled down, so she began.

"Once upon a time there was a goose. Her name was Grace and she had three small goslings. One gosling was bigger than the rest and was always getting in the way. He used to get a bit upset about being told to go and swim over there or to go and play on the other grassy bank. His name was Gregory but they called him Greg for short or sometimes Big Greg. As Greg grew older he began to realise that the other birds on the river were a bit afraid of him, because he was big. Greg knew that he could get his own way by swimming up to the little ducklings and splashing the water. It was one of his favourite tricks.

He would laugh when he scared them and flap his wings with delight as they shrieked and scurried away. If he saw that they had something nice to eat he would dive into the middle of them and gobble up the food. He would do it just for fun, and not because he was hungry. His mother would say to him, Gregory, don't be such a bully. But Gregory took no notice. He had got used to getting his own way. Soon no one liked him. At night-time when all the birds were cuddled up together to keep warm Gregory was told to go away. He had to find a place to sleep alone. He was too big to fit into anyone's bed. Even his own brother and sister said so.

One day Sylvia, the swan, was furious with Gregory and she chased him away. She hissed at him and flapped her wings. She chased him up the grassy bank and over the fields to a different part of the river. Big Greg had been scaring one of her little cygnets that was just learning to swim. The baby cygnet's name was Chloe. That same evening Gregory was quite scared himself. He didn't dare to go back home because he knew how cross Sylvia was with him. Now he was on a strange riverbank. It was growing dark. He could hear noises he didn't understand. He felt frightened and very alone. Gregory began to cry. He ran this way and that way. He swam this way and that way. He tried to get into a hole in the riverbank, but it was too small for him.

"What shall I do?" he wailed.

He cried even more. It was very windy.

Just then a man passed by. He was taking his dog for a walk. He was rather surprised when he saw a goose.

"Goodness me," he said, "What are you doing here?"

Then he noticed Gregory was crying.

"Oh! You poor goose, come home with me. My wife will look after you and so shall I."

So Gregory followed the man all the way back to his house.

The man's little dog thought it was great fun.

It wasn't long before Gregory settled into his new home. The man made a large pen for the goose. He also made a small wooden shelter inside the pen and filled it with fresh straw every day.

"That is a lovely soft bed for you, goose," he would say.

Each day the man's wife would bring Gregory delicious food to eat and fresh water to drink.

"I think the goose should have a pond," said Claire to her husband. His name was Robert. The very next day Robert bought a child's paddling pool and filled it with water.

"There," he said to Gregory, "now you have a wonderful pond to swim in."

To begin with Gregory felt very safe and very happy. It was lovely to be made such a fuss of. The days went by and Gregory was being looked after, but he was beginning to feel rather lonely. He missed the river and his family. He missed the ducks and the coots and the moorhens. He was even missing the swans.

"I wish I hadn't been so rough with them. I wish I hadn't frightened Chloe. I wish I could go back to the river," he said to himself. Gregory was quite unhappy.

Meanwhile, everyone was looking for Gregory. His mother was very upset. She wondered if someone had kidnapped her son. Everyone was asking the same question. Where is Gregory?

Sylvia felt rather guilty and responsible for Gregory's disappearance. She had crossed the field and gone to the other riverbank to see if she could find him, but he was nowhere to be seen.

"We will have to get a search party together," she said.

That evening the search party set out.

Sylvia led the way. After a while she said, "There is only one way to find him before it gets too dark to see. I shall have to fly over the village to look for him."

So that is what she did.

She soon saw Gregory's pen in Claire and Robert's garden, and flew back at great speed to tell everyone the exciting news.

"When everything is quiet in the village tonight and all the people have gone to sleep, I will fly back to Gregory. I will land very silently in the garden. Then I shall break the lock on the pen with my strong beak. Gregory will escape and fly home with me."

She was thrilled at the thought of it all.

Gregory was half asleep when Sylvia arrived. To begin with he thought he was dreaming. Sylvia said, "Don't worry, Gregory. Don't cry or make a noise. I am here to help you to escape."

Gregory was amazed. He was so very happy to see Sylvia and could hardly believe that she had come to help him. They were soon flying home together.

Gregory told Sylvia that it was his best flight he had ever made, and he apologised to her many times and said how sorry he was that he had upset her and her baby. He promised never to do it again. The next day all the birds on the river, all the ducks, all the geese, all the coots and all the moorhens, yes and all the swans, gave a welcome home party for Gregory.

And that is how Gregory came to be the friendliest goose that ever lived."

The children were delighted with Sophie's story and asked her if she had made up any others. She said she had and that she would tell them another, one day.

Lesson 18: April

> **Story:** **The Young Fox**
> **Theme:** **Strangers and Danger**

Synopsis

Sophie, the storyteller, tells a fable of Rozzo the fox who thinks a stranger is someone who looks strange. However a real danger lurks in the darkness. He is good looking but lethal. Rozzo's actions save him from danger and his voice is heard by an uncle who comforts the young fox. The story shows how appearances can be deceptive. It introduces issues of safety and how we can protect ourselves from harm. It is a cautionary archetypal tale, which takes place in a forest.

Objectives

- To recognise what is right and wrong.

- To take part in discussions.

- To recognise that they belong to various groups and communities, such as family and school.

- To listen to and talk about ways of keeping safe.

- To know that family and friends should care for each other.

- To meet and talk with people.

Preparing for the story

The children sit in their places. Each child must have a suitable pencil and crayons. The teacher asks each child to draw a stranger. The object of the lesson is to introduce the concept of 'stranger' which might not be understood by the child, who may think that a stranger is anyone who looks strange rather than someone they do not know. This person may be a woman or a man, pleasant looking etc. At the end of this preparation the teacher collects in the pictures and with their help explains how a 'stranger', in the case of the story to follow, is simply someone who is not known by the child very, very well.

PSHE
3g.

Read the story

After the above activity has been completed the teacher reads the story to the children.

Circle Time discussion

PSHE
2a. 3g.

English 1.
1a, b, c. 2a, c, d.
3a, c.

Question 1 Did Leroy, Linda and the other children learn something from Sophie's story?

Do you think the children knew what was meant by the word 'strangers' in the story? When we say 'Never talk to strangers' what do we mean?

PSHE
2a. 3g.

English 1.
1a, b, c. 2a, c, d.
3a, c.

Question 2 Do you think that Rozzo knew what his mummy meant when she said, 'But be careful not to talk to strangers'?

Did Rozzo think that animals that didn't look a bit like him were strangers? Did he think another fox could not be a stranger because it looked like him? Was he wrong?

PSHE
2a. 3g

English 1.
1a, b, c. 2a, c. d.
3a, c.

Question 3 Should Rozzo have taken the chocolate from the grown-up fox?

Did Rozzo take the chocolate because he thought the grown-up fox was not a stranger? Was he really a stranger? Should you ever take sweets or chocolate or anything at all from a stranger? Should you ever talk to a stranger? Are all people safe to talk to?

PSHE
1c. 2a.

English 1.
1a, b, c. 2a, c, d.
3a, c.

Question 4 In the story was Rozzo ever scared and was the cruel 'stranger' fox ever scared?

Was Rozzo scared? What does it feel like to be scared? Was Rozzo right to shout and scream for help? Was the cruel 'stranger' fox scared of Rozzo's uncle? What did he do when he saw Rozzo's uncle? Which fox did you like?

PSHE
2a, f. 4d.

English 1.
1a, b, c. 2a, c, d.
3a, c.

Question 5 Which people do we know very well? Which people did Leroy and Linda know well?

Do you know your mum, dad, carer, relative, brother or sister very well? Did Leroy and Linda know Sophie and Hope very well?

Question 6 Did Rozzo feel safe at the end of the story?

Was Rozzo with people he knew very well and were they safe to be with? Did Rozzo's uncle help him to keep safe? Do you think that Rozzo's uncle and cousin Russell really cared for Rozzo? How did they show in the story that they care?

PSHE
2a, f. 3g. 4d.

Supplementary ideas

The children sit on the carpet. The teacher reads them other cautionary tales, for example, Red Riding Hood or Goldilocks and the Three Bears.

English I.
2a. 9b.

The headteacher could arrange with the community policeman to talk to the children about 'stranger danger'.

Because of the sensitivity of the subject there are very few supplementary ideas.

Worksheet instructions

"Josh is taking Leroy and Linda on a woodland walk. He shows them how to make a trail so that they know their way through the woods and back home another time. Can you help Leroy and Linda through the woods and back to the safety of their own home? Now colour the picture."

The Young Fox

Sophie Sellars and her guide dog, Hope, often gave talks at Leroy and Linda's school. They were excellent talks. They were good to listen to, and full of yarns and tales. She had become a storyteller to the children.

Today she was coming to school to talk to the infant class.

"Tell us a story, tell us a story," chanted all the children when they saw Sophie and Hope cross the playground.

"What do you want a story about?" laughed Sophie.

"Wriggly worms," shouted Linda.

"No, no, creepy crawlies," yelled Leroy.

"I think sausages that walk and talk," joked Paul.

"What strange children you are," laughed Sophie, "and that is what my story is going to be about. It is going to be about strangers."

When the children were all assembled together in the hall Sophie began her tale.

"This is a story about keeping safe," Sophie began. "It is a story about Rozzo the Fox."

"Once upon a time there was a young fox called Rozzo. Rozzo felt rather lonely because all the older foxes were playing and they wouldn't let Rozzo join in their game. They said it was because he was too young.

"I would like to play with my cousin," thought Rozzo. He went inside his house to tell his mum. He explained to her that he had nobody to play with and his mummy listened very sympathetically, then he asked her if he could go and play with his cousin, Russell. His mummy said that if he went to see Russell (who lived on the other side of the woods) he would have to be very careful not to talk to strangers.

"I will," said Rozzo, "and am I allowed to play on Russell's bike?"

"Yes," said his mummy. "But be very careful not to speak to strangers."

"I will," said Rozzo. "And if Russell asks me to stay for my tea, may I?"

"Yes," said his mummy. "But be very careful not to speak to strangers."

"Am I allowed to ask Russell to come and play with me one day?" asked Rozzo.

"Yes," said his mummy. "But you must be very careful not to speak to strangers."

So Rozzo set off through the woods to Russell's house. He was just passing some thick bushes when he saw a hedgehog.

"I wonder if he is a stranger," thought Rozzo. "He looks quite strange to me. I had better not speak to him." So Rozzo went on his way.

The next thing that he saw was a squirrel.

"I wonder if he is a stranger?" thought Rozzo. "Perhaps he is. He is a funny grey colour, not at all like me. I think I will just ignore him." So Rozzo went on his way.

The next thing he saw was a rabbit. "I wonder if he is a stranger," thought Rozzo. "It certainly hasn't got much of a tail. It's not a bit like me."

So Rozzo didn't speak to the rabbit and continued on his way.

He was just about to enter the tree-lined driveway to Russell's house when he saw a grown-up fox.

This fox looked very much like his dad. He was about the same size.

"He can't be a stranger," thought Rozzo. "He looks very much like one of our family."

"Where are you going to, little fox?" asked the grown-up fox.

"I am going to my cousin's," answered Rozzo. "They are expecting me."

"Would you like a lovely piece of my chocolate?" the grown-up fox said.

"Oh! Yes, please," said Rozzo. He was just about to take a piece of chocolate when the large fox grabbed hold of him.

Rozzo was very scared and he wriggled and shouted so loudly that all the crows in the trees started to squawk and fly about overhead.

Rozzo's Uncle, who was gathering wood, heard the noise. Russell was with him.

"What are those crows making such a fuss about?" Russell asked his dad.

He was rather surprised when his dad shouted, "Follow me," and ran off very quickly down the tree-lined drive.

Rozzo, who was being dragged off the path by the cruel fox, saw his Uncle and his little cousin running towards him.

"Help!" screamed Rozzo.

But Rozzo was safe again because the cruel fox ran off leaving Rozzo behind and free. This time the cruel fox was scared. He didn't want Rozzo's Uncle to catch him, and he didn't want Rozzo's Uncle to know who he was.

Rozzo was very relieved to be safe and he told his cousin all about the bad fox and the offer of chocolate.

Rozzo's Uncle said that the bad fox was a stranger because Rozzo didn't know him.

"Don't talk to foxes that you don't know very, very well," he ordered.

"Yes," said Russell. "I talk only to foxes that I know very, very well. Foxes who are my cousins or my aunties or my uncles."

"Strangers don't have to look strange," Russell explained. "They are often foxes that look very much like us. They often look very nice and friendly. But we don't know them and we don't know what they will do, so we don't talk to them at all."

"Yes," said his Uncle. "Russell is right. We have to protect ourselves from strangers. Not all foxes are good foxes."

"So, now, from that day to this Rozzo never speaks to strangers and he never, ever, takes chocolates or sweets from them."

"And that is the end of my story about strangers," said Sophie.

"I never speak to people that are strangers," said Leroy.

"I never speak to people that are strangers," said Linda.

"Strangers might look very nice people and offer you chocolates," said Paul. "But I never speak to them because they might be dangerous."

"Yes, they might hurt me," said Rosie.

And all the other children said, "Yes, and me too!"

Lesson 19: May

> **Story:** The Exciting Day
> **Theme:** Excitement

Synopsis

The story looks at the issue of choosing between good things and deals with the question of economics. Excitement can be scary too, as Leroy learns when he gets lost in the cinema. The story ends when Leroy is found and receives a tear stained kiss from Mum.

Objectives

- To share their opinions on things that matter to them and explain their views.

- To recognise, name and deal with their feelings.

- To take part in discussion.

- To recognise choices they can make.

- To understand that they belong to families.

- To understand what improves and harms their local and built environment.

- To realise that money comes from different sources and can be used for different purposes.

- To understand that there are people who can help them stay safe.

- To understand that family and friends should care for one another.

Preparing for the story

The teacher tells the children that they can choose between two rewards or good things. (What those rewards or good things are should be flexible for the teacher to decide and must comply with the rules of the school). Here is a list of suggestions:

A nature or other observational walk.

An extra star on the chart.

The children can make their own puppet show.

Make a shop in the classroom.

For example the two good things may be a nature walk and make a shop in the classroom. The children are asked to vote for one of the two good things. The teacher makes a block graph of the results. The teacher explains that sometimes treats cost money. Ask the children to think of times when the children receive gifts. What are they? They might be:

presents for birthdays or Christmas
money from relatives in the holidays
holiday money
pocket money.

PSHE
2a, c.

Tell them that you are going to read a story where children had to make a choice between two good things, but something happens which surprises them and they have more choices than they thought.

Read the story

After the above activity has been completed the teacher reads the story to the children.

Circle Time discussion

PSHE
Ic. 2a ,c.

English I.
Ia, b, c. 2a, c, d.
3a, c.

Question I At the beginning of the story the children were asked to choose between two good things. How did it make them feel?

Did they feel sad and angry or happy and excited? Have you ever had to choose between treats? Is it a hard thing to do? Do you think Leroy and Linda thought it was a hard thing to do? Would you have chosen the cinema or the burger bar?

PSHE
Ic. 2a, c, i.

English I.
Ia, b, c. 2a, c, d.
3a, c.

Question 2 The children got a letter and money from their grandparents. Did they now have more choices?

Was it a kind thing of their grandparents to do? Do you think it would make the children feel happy or sad? Could the children now have both good things? Do you think they were lucky? Why did Brenda say, "It looks as if you two have got your own way after all"?

Question 3 Did Leroy get lost on purpose and how do you think he felt?

PSHE
1c.

English 1.
1a, b, c. 2a, c. d.
3a, c.

What happened to make Leroy get lost? Did mummy and Linda have to look for Linda's hat? Did Leroy get pushed out with the crowd? Did Leroy feel upset that he was lost? Did he feel like crying? Have you ever felt like crying?

Question 4 Leroy asked a policeman to help him. Do you think that was a good idea? What did Leroy know that helped him?

PSHE
2a. 3g.

English 1.
1a, b, c. 2a, c, d.
3a, c.

Did Leroy have to ask for someone's help? Did he know the other people? Did the policeman help Leroy keep safe? Did the policeman take him to the police station? Was that a safe place to go? Did Leroy know his name, address and telephone number? Do you know your name, address and telephone number? What is it?

Question 5 When mummy, daddy and Linda heard that Leroy was at the police station what did they do and why did mummy cry?

PSHE
2a, f. 4d.

English 1.
1a, b, c. 2a, c, d.
3a, c.

Did they rush to the police station? Do you think they were glad to find Leroy? Was mummy pleased to find Leroy? Was she happy? How do you know she felt happy? Did she cry tears of joy?

Question 6 Have you ever been lost? What happened?

PSHE
1c. 2f. 4d.

English 1.
1a, b, c. 2a, c, d.
3a, c.

How did you feel when you were lost? Did anyone help you? What did people who you know very well (family and friends) do? How do you think they might have felt?

Supplementary ideas

The children sit in groups of four with pencils and crayons. They are each given a piece of A4 paper divided into two. The teacher asks them what sorts of things they like doing for a treat. Do treats make them happy and excited? Perhaps they have some special food. Leroy and Linda loved cheeseburgers, milkshakes and ice cream. Leroy and Linda liked going to the cinema. Does going to the cinema make the children excited? Perhaps they like going to the zoo or the seaside for a treat? Maybe they have had a ride on an animal that made them happy and excited. Now the children should draw two things which are a treat to them. The children, (perhaps with the help of an adult providing a model) write a caption under their picture such as:

'Pizzas with cheese make me happy.'
'Building sandcastles makes me happy.'

'Playing football makes me happy.'

The teacher or adult helper assembles the pictures into a class book with captions such as:

'Trips to the zoo and fish and chips make Kenneth happy.'

At a separate time the teacher reads the book to the whole class.

PSHE
1b. 2a. 4c.

English 1.
1a, b, c. 2a, d. 3a, e.

English 3.
1c. 4e.

The children are gathered onto the carpet for a discussion. The teacher discusses buildings and their environments with the children. The teacher explains to the children that Leroy and Linda were familiar with the cinema building and the 'Burger Shed'. They also went to the police station. The teacher asks the children if there are any buildings that they are familiar with. The teacher has a large sheet of paper on which she makes a chart of the buildings that the children know. She puts ticks by each building to represent how many children are familiar with that building. At a later date the teacher could make a block graph with the information gathered during this discussion for display and discussion with the children. The buildings known to the children could include schools, different shops, fire station, police station, hospital, hairdressers, churches and libraries. The teacher could ask the children whether there were any rules or codes of conduct in different buildings. For example, are we quiet in churches and libraries? Would we go to a police station if we were lost? The teacher could also ask the children what sort of things might harm the buildings, for example graffiti, vandalism, litter, little maintenance, theft, lightning, floods, subsidence, fire or wood rot.

PSHE
2a. 2g.

Geography
1c.

The teacher obtains a number of hats or artefacts of people who help us. They may include policemen, teachers, nurses, doctors and firemen. In pairs volunteer children act out a scene where one child is the helper and the other the helped. For example a policeman might say, "Are you lost?" and the one who is helped might say, "I can't find my mummy and daddy." (Puppets could also be used.)

PSHE
3g.

English 1.
4a, b.

The teacher will need a copy of each child's address and a postcard for each child. The teacher gathers together the children on the carpet. She talks about the importance of children's addresses. The children are asked individually what their name and address is. The children can then be given a postcard to write their name and address on. Children with special needs or younger children could order their address, which has previously been written out and cut into strips by the teacher or assistant.

Worksheet instructions

"Look at the worksheet of a cinema screen and some people watching a film. What film are they watching? Think hard for a moment. There is one empty seat. Can you find it? Later you will draw yourself sitting in the empty seat. I wonder who you might be sitting next to. Now draw a scene from a film on the screen and draw yourself in the seat, and then you can colour your picture."

(After the children have done this the teacher explains the other worksheet, which is a dot-to-dot):

"You are going to join the dots on the glass. There is a milk-shake in the glass. Later you will choose a flavour and colour the milkshake in the correct colour. Perhaps pink for straw-berry or brown for chocolate or some other flavour and colour of your own choosing. Join the dots on the cheeseburger and on Brenda's cheesecake. Colour them in the correct colour. Now think of a drink that you would choose and draw it in one of the squares. Think of something you would choose to eat and draw it in the other square. Now colour the picture."

(N.B. The emphasis is put on choice.)

Lesson 19

The Exciting Day

The half-term school holidays had just begun and Brenda wondered if she should take the twins to the cinema. They had never been to the cinema and she knew that the children's film was good and every child she knew had enjoyed it.

"I will take you for a treat on Wednesday," said Brenda to the twins. "That is my day off from work. You may choose between going to the cinema or going to the Burger Shed for tea."

"I want both," shouted Linda, happily.

"Yes, both, both, both," Leroy shouted as he rushed up to his mummy and gave her a big hug.

"No. You must decide on just one treat for that day," their mummy said.

She spoke in a very firm way and the twins knew that when their mummy spoke like that she meant it and that there was no point in arguing with her. So Leroy and Linda said that they were going to have one of their 'private meetings' about it. They went into a corner of the living room and began to whisper to each other. It was a hard choice for them to make. They loved going to the Burger Shed. They thought the cheeseburgers were 'yummy!' and the milkshakes and the puddings 'fantastic'.

"I like the apple pudding in parcel packets," whispered Linda loudly and said "Mmmm!"

"I think ice cream, with strawberry juice on top, a big heap of it too, is what I shall have," Leroy announced in an even louder whisper.

"Yes and mummy will ask for cheesecake," Linda added. "She always likes that."

"But I want to go to the cinema," said Leroy.

"Me too!" yelled Linda.

"Now, treats are treats and sometimes people have to choose between two good things," said Brenda, who was growing tired of waiting for the twins to decide.

"I think," said Linda and then after a long pause, "THE CINEMA!"

Then Leroy shouted, "Yes, THE CINEMA, THE CINEMA!"

When Wednesday came Leroy and Linda were very happy and they shouted goodbye to Josh, their dad, as he set off on his bike to work.

"Tell me all about the film this evening," he said, "and be good children for your mummy."

As he was riding away the postman arrived.

There was one letter for Jenny, the twins' big sister, and another letter that was addressed to Leroy and Linda. In each envelope there was a new ten pound note. The money was a gift from their grandparents.

Brenda read the letter to the twins.

"Dear Linda and Leroy,

Here is some money for you to spend in the half-term holidays. Be careful not to lose the money.

Have a good time.

With lots of love from

Huff and Puff xxx"

"Now we can go to the Burger Shed. Now we can go to the Burger Shed," the twins sang excitedly.

"Daddy can come as well," Leroy said.

Brenda laughed, "It looks as if you two have got your own way after all. All right, I will ring daddy after we have seen the film. He will be back home by then. I will ask him to come and meet us outside the cinema."

Leroy and Linda were very happy but when they got inside the cinema and realised that it was so dark they were a little worried. However, they soon got used to it and they enjoyed watching the film on the big screen. They loved the film because it was exciting.

They didn't want the film to end but knew it had because all the people and all the children in the cinema left their seats and started to push their way to the doors marked 'EXIT'.

Linda's woolly hat had slipped off her knee and fallen under the seat in front of hers.

"My hat," she cried, "my hat."

It was while Linda and mummy were trying to pick up Linda's hat that an awful thing happened. Leroy had been pushed forward with the crowd of people leaving the cinema and before he realised he was outside on the street and mummy and Linda were nowhere to be found. Leroy was very worried. Inside the cinema mummy and Linda were very worried too.

"Leroy, Leroy, where are you?" they called.

"Mummy, mummy, where are you?" Leroy called as he walked down the street searching for them.

Mummy and Linda were getting very upset because Leroy was not in the cinema.

Leroy was also getting very upset because he could not see mummy and Linda and there were so many people walking down the road. Leroy tried to be brave but it was very hard not to cry. He wondered if he should tell somebody that he was lost but all the people were strangers to him and Leroy had been told not to speak to strangers. Then he saw a tall man with black boots, and as he looked up he saw the man was wearing dark blue trousers, a dark blue jacket and a helmet. It was a policeman.

"Please, please, I have lost my mummy and my sister," said Leroy in a timid little voice as he tapped the policeman on his leg.

"Oh dear," said the policeman. "We had better find them for you. Come over to the police station with me and we will see what we can do."

At the police station Leroy was asked if he knew his name and address. Of course, Leroy knew that and he also knew his telephone number.

The police rang and Josh answered the phone and said he would come down to the police station straight away.

Then the policeman telephoned the cinema and the next thing that Brenda and Linda heard was a voice coming over the loud speaker in the cinema.

"If Brenda and Linda are in the cinema could they come down to the police station where Leroy is waiting for them."

Josh rushed to the police station and mummy and Linda rushed to the police station. They all arrived at the police station at the same time and there they found Leroy sitting on a table and wearing a policeman's helmet. He was eating biscuits and drinking a glass of milk.

"There are some people here to see you," the policeman said to Leroy. "Do you think you know them?" The policeman laughed, Leroy laughed, Linda laughed and Josh laughed. It was only Brenda who didn't laugh. Instead she began to cry.

"Why did you cry, when you saw me at the police station, mummy?" asked Leroy as he was tucking into his meal in the Burger Shed.

"Yes, why did you cry, mummy?" asked Linda. "I didn't cry, I was happy to see Leroy."

"Those were tears of joy," said Josh. "Mummy cried because she was so very happy."

"Was she happier than I am eating my cheeseburger?" asked Leroy taking a big bite.

"Happier than all the cheeseburgers in the world," answered Brenda as she wiped the tomato sauce off Leroy's face and gave him a kiss.

Lesson 20: May

Story: The Little Black Kitten
Theme: Honesty and Lies

Synopsis

Linda disclaims all knowledge and lies about her involvement with a little black kitten, a bucket and some fish. All ends well when the missing things are found and Linda vows never to tell lies again. This is a story about dishonesty and its consequences.

Objectives

- To recognise what they like and dislike, what is fair and unfair and what is right and wrong.

- To take part in discussion.

- To recognise how their behaviour affects other people.

- To understand that family and friends should care for one another.

Preparing for the story

The children sit in a circle and Circle Time conventions are adopted. The teacher explains to the children that he will start the discussion with the phrase:

"If I broke my mother's favourite vase I would…" (He completes the sentence).

Now the children complete the sentence. When this is done every-one in turn completes the following sentence:

"If I borrowed a book or a toy from a friend and then I lost it I would…"

PSHE
1a. 2a. 4a, d.

English 1.
1a, b, c. 2a, c, d.
3a, c.

Read the story

After the above activity has been completed the teacher reads the story to the children.

Circle Time discussion

PSHE
2a. 4d.

English I.
Ia, b, c. 2a, c, d.
3a, c.

Question I Do you think that Linda was bored and lonely when Leroy was poorly?

Did Linda want a friend? Was she pleased to see the kitten? Did she want to keep the kitten as her friend?

PSHE
Ia. 2a.

English I.
Ia, b, c. 2a, c, d.
3a, c.

Question 2 Did Linda tell lies in the story? Is it right or wrong to tell lies?

What lies did Linda tell? Who did she tell lies too? Why do you think she told lies to her daddy, mummy and Shama?

PSHE
2a. 4a.

English I.
Ia, b, c. 2a, c. d.
3a, c.

Question 3 How do you think other people felt when Linda told lies to them?

How do you think that Shama felt when she couldn't find her little black kitten? Do you think that she was worried? How do you think that mum and dad felt when they couldn't find their bucket and fish?

PSHE
2a. 4a.

English I.
Ia, b, c. 2a, c, d.
3a, c.

Question 4 What things happened because Linda told lies?

What did daddy (Josh) have to buy? Did he have to buy a bucket and some fish? Do you think he was pleased?

PSHE
Ia. 2a.

English I.
Ia, b, c. 2a, c, d.
3a, c.

Question 5 How do you think Linda felt when she told the lies?

Did Linda go to bed after she told the lies? Why do you think she did that? Do you think she felt happy and strong or unhappy? How do you think she felt after she couldn't find the bucket, fish or little black kitten?

PSHE
Ia. 2a.

English I.
Ia, b, c. 2a, c, d.
3a, c.

Question 6 Linda gave her daddy her spending money and said she was sorry to Shama. Do you think this was fair?

Why do you think it was fair or unfair? Do you think Linda felt happier when she had done these things?

Supplementary ideas

The teacher tells the children that everyone needs to have privacy and sometimes secrets are good. The children are arranged for an art lesson and provided with collage material, glue and an undecorated box. They decorate their box and then make a small clay model of their own to put in the box and to take home.

PSHE
1a.

Art & Design
5c.

The teacher tells the children the following anecdote:

> "Sue wanted some friends, she thought that making up stories was a good way to make friends. She kept rushing up to other children in the playground and telling them that one of their friends was hurt, and then when they looked and found their friend they were not hurt at all. One day a girl called Sali hurts herself in the playground. She had hurt herself, badly. Sue saw this and ran to tell Sali's friends but no one believed Sue and she had to cry before she was believed. Sue realised that she had told so many lies about people being hurt that no one believed her when it really happened."

The teacher asks the children if other people could trust Sue? Do you think that Sue was right when she thought that telling lies or stories was a good idea, and a good way to make friends?

PSHE
1a. 2a.

The children are asked by the teacher to think of good and bad behaviour towards kittens, and some good and bad behaviour of kittens towards people. Together, teacher and children investigate the following unfinished sentences providing some appropriate ideas.

Some people are good to kittens and they…	(remember to feed them regularly and give them drinks etc.)
Some people are not good to kittens, they…	(forget to feed them, do not provide them with water, put them in in buckets, pull their tail etc.)
Some kittens get up to tricks and they…	(steal food and other cats' toys, climb up curtains etc.)
Some kittens are good and they…	(purr when they are stroked, are friendly and kind, do not spill their food or drink, do not scratch etc.)

PSHE
1a. 2a.

Worksheet instructions

"On the worksheet you will see a picture of an apple, a kitten, a bird, a fish, an elephant and a bucket. Which of these things were in the story about the little black kitten? The first thing you can see is an apple. If you think it is true that an apple was in the story put a tick in the circle; if you do not think it was true put a cross in the circle. When you have finished you can colour the pictures."

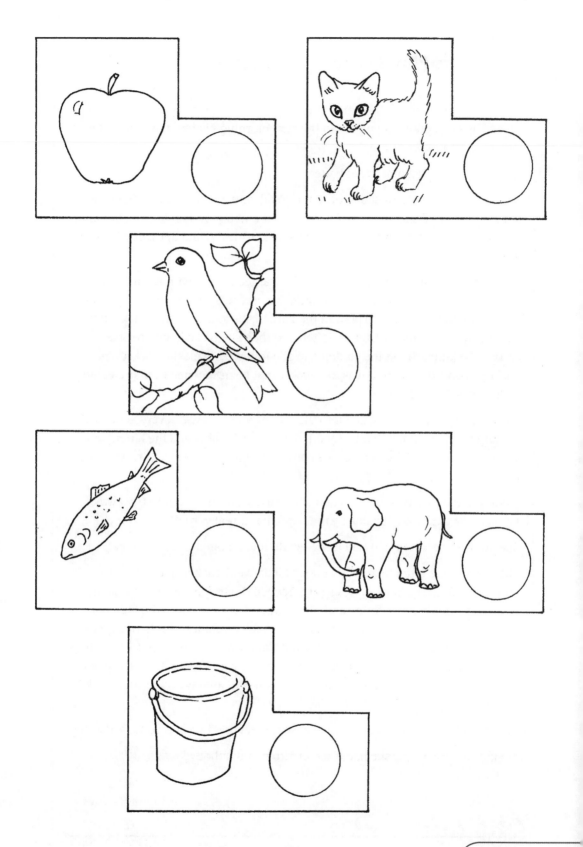

The Little Black Kitten

Leroy had been poorly all night. So the next morning his mummy said, "Stay in bed, Leroy, and keep warm."

His mummy wanted him to get better.

She took some books upstairs for him to read, and his new comic. Then she made him a hot drink and two pieces of toast and honey. Leroy felt better after that and asked his mummy to read him some stories. A bit later Leroy fell fast asleep.

Linda wanted somebody to play with. She wanted to play with Leroy but Leroy was in bed. Leroy was not well. So when mummy was reading to Leroy, Linda went out into the garden to play. In the garden she saw the little black kitten. Linda played with the little black kitten and then she picked him up. She carried the kitten round the garden and she found a big plastic bucket. The bucket belonged to Josh. It was the bucket that he used when he was cleaning windows in The Crescent.

Linda put the little black kitten into the bucket and as it was a very large bucket the kitten could not climb out. Then Linda hid the bucket and the kitten under some thick bushes at the end of the garden. The bushes were behind the shed in the garden.

Linda wanted to keep the kitten and she didn't want the kitten to run away. Linda knew that it was Shama's kitten and that it really lived next door.

She stroked the kitten and told it she would find it something nice to eat.

She thought the kitten might be hungry. Linda went back inside her house and she went to the kitchen. There she opened the fridge and she saw some fish. Linda took the fish to the end of the garden and gave it to the little black kitten to eat. It was a very big fish. Mummy had bought it to cook for supper. The kitten loved the fish and ate some but there was far too much for one little kitten to eat. Linda left the fish in the bucket, she said "There, I will leave you the fish so that you won't go hungry. I like you. You are my secret little black kitten."

But the kitten did not hear Linda because it had curled up and gone fast asleep.

Linda was very happy, she had a secret kitten and nobody knew.

Linda went into the house again and closed the door. She started to look at her books about kittens. Then there was a knock at the front door. It was Shama. Mummy opened the door.

"Hello! Shama," she said. "Come in."

"Have you seen my little black kitten?" asked Shama.

"No," said mummy.

Shama looked at Linda.

"Have you seen my little black kitten?" she asked.

"No," said Linda.

Poor Shama was sad, she was very worried.

"I will have to go and find it," she said. "I hope it's not lost."

Then Linda's daddy came home.

He was looking for his big plastic bucket.

"Have you seen my bucket?" asked Josh.

"No," said Brenda.

"Well, have you seen my big plastic bucket Linda?" he asked.

"No," said Linda.

Josh had to go to the shop to buy another big plastic bucket. He thought the other one was lost.

He did not ask Leroy because Leroy was fast asleep.

Mummy went to the kitchen. She said she would make a nice supper.

But where was the fish?

"Have you seen the fish?" she asked Josh.

"No," said Josh.

"Have you seen the fish?" she asked Linda.

"No," said Linda.

Mummy was very puzzled. She tried to think about where she could have put the fish. All the thinking gave her a headache.

Josh had to go to the shop AGAIN. Josh had to buy some more fish.

Linda didn't want to tell anybody about her secret, so she went upstairs to her bed. Very soon Linda fell asleep.

Leroy woke up. He had had a long sleep. He was feeling better.

He thought he heard a noise. He had heard a noise and it was a 'miaow'.

Leroy went downstairs. Mummy and Josh were watching television. They had not heard the little black kitten miaowing.

Leroy told them what he had heard.

Josh got a torch and he went into the garden to see if he could find the little black kitten. Mummy and Leroy went too.

Then Josh heard the miaow and mummy heard the miaow.

"Where is it?" asked Josh.

"Where is it?" asked mummy.

"It's here," said Leroy. "It's in Josh's bucket."

"Goodness," said mummy.

"Goodness," said Josh.

"Goodness," said Leroy. "There's a big piece of fish in the bucket as well."

Mummy carried the little black kitten back to Shama's house. Shama was very happy.

Josh washed his bucket. He didn't want his bucket to have a fishy smell. He wrapped the fish in some paper and said that Shama could have it to give to the little black kitten and her other cats. So Leroy took the fish to Shama's house. Shama was happy.

The next morning Linda got up early. She went straight to the garden to look for the little black kitten but it was not there. She looked for the bucket but the bucket was not there. She looked and looked in the bushes but she couldn't find the bucket or the little black kitten.

Linda began to cry.

"Has anybody seen the bucket?" asked Linda.

"Yes," said Josh.

"Well, has anybody seen the little black kitten?" she cried.

"Yes," said mummy.

"Yes, they have," said Leroy, "and mummy and Josh don't tell lies."

Later they told Linda about what had happened when she was asleep. Linda was very sorry for what she had done. She knew Shama had been sad and she knew Josh had had to spend some more money because he had to buy another bucket and some more fish.

"I will give you my spending money this week," said Linda, "and I will tell Shama that I am sorry."

"Well I am sure Shama will let you play with the little black kitten," said mummy.

Linda went up to her mummy and mummy gave her a hug. Then Linda whispered, "I'm sorry mummy, and I will never tell lies again."

Lesson 21: June

> **Story:** **The Mystery Thief**
> **Theme:** **Stealing**

Synopsis

Who is stealing? Who is the thief in The Crescent? Who is causing mayhem? At last the thief is caught. It is Frisky the dog! The story deals with the consequences of stealing and the question of culpability and intention.

Objectives

- To recognise what the children like and dislike, what is fair and unfair, and what is right and wrong.

- To share their opinions on things that matter to them.

- To recognise and name their feelings.

- To know that they belong to communities such as school.

- To recognise that their behaviour affects others.

- To take and share responsibility.

- To develop relationships through work.

Preparing for the story

The teacher has the following objects: a rubber bone, a toy duck, a play mat, two apples and a pineapple and a small wheel or a truck. The teacher holds up the objects and the children guess which person in The Crescent they belong to. She can also hold up the initial letter.

H	(A rubber bone - Hope the dog)
Z	(A play mat - baby Zoë)
L	(A toy duck - Linda)
Mr A	(Two apples and a pineapple - Mr Allsorts)
P	(Small wheel or truck - Paul)
J	(Bucket and wash leather - Josh)

PSHE
2a.

217

Read the story

After the above activity has been completed the teacher reads the story to the children.

Circle Time discussion

Question 1 How did the people in The Crescent feel when they discovered some of their things had gone missing?

PSHE
1a. 2a.

English 1.
1a, b, c. 2a, c, d.
3a, c.

Did it cause confusion? Was Leroy angry when Linda said that he knew where her toy duck had gone? Was it nice to think there must be a thief in The Crescent? Was Paul worried about his truck? Did it make the residents sad or happy? Does your behaviour affect others?

PSHE
1a, b. 2a.

English 1.
1a, b, c. 2a, c, d.
3a, c.

Question 2 Paul said that it is wrong to steal. Was Paul correct?

Why is it wrong to steal other people's things? Why do you think that some people steal?

PSHE
1a. 2a.

English 1.
1a, c. 2a, c. d.
3a, c.

Question 3 Did Frisky know the difference between right and wrong?

Did Frisky know that he had upset people? Was he upset when Shama shouted at him? Do you think he would do it again? Was he a naughty or a good puppy? Do you know the difference between right and wrong?

PSHE
1a, c. 2a.

English 1.
1a, c. 2a, c, d.
3a, c.

Question 4 Have you ever had something stolen from you, or have you ever lost something and thought it was stolen? How did you feel?

Is it worrying when something is stolen? Do you like it when something goes missing? Do you not like it? How does it make you feel?

Question 5 Did the people of The Crescent take care of their things? Is it right to take care of your things?

Should you be able to leave things in you garden? If so what type of things? Is it best to leave things in a safe place? Might leaving things in your garden tempt others to steal?

PSHE
2a, c. 4a.

English 1.
1a, c. 2a, c, d.
3a, c.

Question 6 Is borrowing the same thing as stealing?

If someone said you could borrow his or her crayons is that all right? If you didn't give the crayons back on purpose would that be a good thing to do? If someone gave you a sweet is that a good thing to do? If someone took your crisps and ate them would that be stealing?

PSHE
1a. 2a, c.

English 1.
1a, c. 2a, c, d.
3a, c.

Supplementary ideas

The teacher makes a 'borrowing table'. It may contain rubbers, pencils, crayons, counters, rulers, chalks and weighing scales. The teacher tells the children that she trusts them all to return the things they have borrowed. The teacher tells the children they are for borrowing and they must bring them back at the end of the lesson. The teacher asks the children which lesson they might need the things for.

PSHE
2f. 5a, f.

Read the story of Goldilocks and the Three Bears. Was Goldilocks wrong to eat baby bear's porridge? Do you think she knew it was wrong? Do you think she might have been sorry? How could Goldilocks make it better for baby bear? The children make a card for baby bear because he lost his porridge.

PSHE
1a, c. 2a.

The teacher gathers the children around her. She has previously written the following items (which children and teacher match together).

A fire station	A computer
A school	A policeman's helmet
A flower shop	Daffodils
A police station	A comic
A jewellers shop	A hosepipe
A newsagent	A ring

The teacher tells the children that there is a thief in town. He has taken away some things and does not intend to give them back. He is using them for himself. Is it wrong or right to steal? The teacher then reads the name of a building (the first one is a fire station). She asks the children what the thief might steal from that building, a computer, a policeman's helmet, some daffodils, a comic, a hosepipe or a ring. The children put up their hands and when someone gives the correct answer the teacher joins the two items with a line. She continues until all buildings and items stolen are joined correctly.

Worksheet instructions

"You are going to match the things or articles which were stolen by Frisky. He went into other people's gardens, and took their things away. He didn't know that he was stealing but he was. He didn't know that the people of The Crescent were going round and round in circles looking for the things that belonged to them. Match the stolen articles by drawing a nice straight line from the bucket to the bucket, the play mat to the play mat, the wheel to the wheel, the apples to the apples, the bone to the bone and the toy duck to the toy duck. When you have done this you can colour the picture."

The Mystery Thief

At Number 8 The Crescent there was something missing.

"Where is my best toy duck?" cried Linda.

"Leroy, have you taken Linda's toy duck?" shouted Brenda, their mum, angrily.

"No, I have not taken her duck. I don't know where it is. Linda keeps telling me I do know but I don't," Leroy shouted. He was very cross.

At Number 1 The Crescent Sali could not find Zoë's play mat anywhere. She had put it in the garden, but now it had gone.

"I think we must have had robbers," said Sali to her husband, Tim.

"That's very strange," said Tim. "Who would want to take a play mat?"

"Strange things do happen," Sali replied.

At Morningdale Court, Hope, Sophie's guide dog, had lost her rubber bone. Hope was looking for her rubber bone.

"Oh dear!" said Brenda, when Sophie told her about the bone. "Everything seems to be missing today. I think we must have a thief in The Crescent."

At the corner shop, in The Crescent, two apples and a pineapple had been taken from Mr. Allsorts' fruit display. He was upset and thought that a shoplifter had taken them.

"Wait until I catch the thief," he warned.

At Number 7 The Crescent, Paul was looking for the wheel from his truck.

"I left it on the grass at the front of the house," said Paul to his grandma. "Now it's gone. It has just disappeared."

Grandma tried to help Paul to find the wheel, but it was nowhere to be seen."

"How very peculiar," said grandma. "We will have to ask your dad if he took it to work with him, by mistake."

"I think there must be thief about," said Paul. He was worried; his truck was no use with only three wheels.

Soon everybody was hunting up and down The Crescent. They were all looking for their lost belongings.

"I think we must have had a thief in The Crescent," said Josh. He was looking for his small plastic bucket and his wash leather.

"I was going to clean the windows at Morningdale Court, and I had left my bucket in the driveway. Now it's gone," said Josh angrily.

At Number 9 The Crescent, Shama couldn't find her puppy dog, Frisky.

"Has anybody seen Frisky?" shouted Shama. "I think he must have escaped from the back garden. I hope he hasn't been stolen. He's such a friendly puppy and he would go off with anybody."

Shama was very concerned and she was shouting "Frisky! Frisky!" as loudly as she could.

Now everybody was searching for their own things and they were also searching for Frisky.

Jenny and Susie, who were just returning home from the recreation ground, heard all the people calling for Frisky.

"We've found him. We've found him," they shouted. "Don't worry, Shama. Frisky is alright."

Everybody turned to look and there, much to their surprise, they saw Jenny and Susie. Jenny was holding onto Frisky's collar and Susie had her arms full of things.

"We found him playing on the recreation ground with all these things," said Jenny. She was breathless and so was Susie. Frisky too was panting but still looking very playful.

"That's my bucket," yelled Josh.

"That's my duck," screeched Linda.

"That's my bone," woofed Hope.

"That's Zoe's play mat," said Sali.

"That's the wheel from my truck," laughed Paul.

"That's my rather chewed up fruit," smiled Mr. Allsorts. "I can't sell that now."

"And that's my naughty dog," said Shama. "Don't wander off again," she scolded.

"And here's the thief," said Susie's granddad, who had come out to see if he could help to solve the mystery.

Frisky wagged his tail. He had been having such a wonderful time playing with all the things that he had stolen.

"You are a naughty dog," said Shama. "You mustn't steal. You have upset everybody."

Frisky had never heard Shama shout at him before, and he hung his head. He knew he had done something wrong.

"Never mind," said Paul, giving Frisky a pat. "Dogs don't know that it is very wrong to steal but it is."

Frisky gave Paul a lick as if to say, 'thank you for forgiving me.'

"I think we should call that dog Mystery, not Frisky," laughed Paul, and he threw a ball into Shama's garden for him to chase.

"Fetch, Mystery," shouted Paul.

Everybody laughed and took their own things back to their homes.

Lesson 22: June

> **Story:** **The Plums**
> **Theme:** **Guilt**

Synopsis

This story deals with the temptation to steal and the desire to hide the evidence. It touches on the feelings of those who have transgressed and the need to confess and be forgiven. Laughter is a good device for neutralising feelings of guilt and encouraging forgiveness.

Objectives

- To recognise what they like and dislike.

- To share their opinions on things that matter to them and explain their views.

- To recognise, name and deal with feelings in a positive way.

- To take part in discussion.

- To recognise choices they can make and recognise the difference between right and wrong.

- To understand that household products and medicine can be harmful if not used properly.

- To know that family and friends should care for one another.

Preparing for the story

The teacher gathers the children onto the carpet. She tells the children that if we do something wrong we feel guilty. The children have to put their hands on their heads if the answer is Yes and fold their arms if the answer is No. The teacher asks the children the following questions:

- Do we feel guilty if we steal someone's lunch?

- Do we feel guilty if it is a sunny day and we are playing outside?

- Do we feel guilty if we borrow someone's crayon and don't give it back?

- Do we feel guilty if it's Monday morning and we are getting ready for school?

Read the story

After the above activity has been completed the teacher reads the story to the children.

Circle Time discussion

PSHE
1a. 2a.

English 1.
1a, b, c. 2a, c, d.
3a, c.

Question 1 What did Leroy do which was wrong?

Why do you think Leroy ate Linda's plum? Was he stealing Linda's plum? Is this a wrong thing to do? Can you understand why Leroy stole the plum?

PSHE
2a, c.

English 1.
1a, b, c. 2a, c, d.
3a, c.

Question 2 Why did Leroy try to hide himself under the hydrangea bush and why did he try to hide the plum stone?

Did Leroy have the choice to eat the plum or not to eat the plum? Did Leroy want to hide the evidence and pretend he did not really eat the plum? Did Leroy want to hide himself because he felt guilty?

PSHE
1b. 2a.

English 1.
1a, b, c. 2a, c. d.
3a, c.

Question 3 Why did Leroy not want to play? Why did he go to sleep?

Is it hard to play when you are thinking about other things? What do you think? Did Leroy go to sleep because he wanted to forget what he had done?

Question 4 Did Leroy feel better when he told Linda and mummy what he had done? Do you think Linda and mummy loved Leroy?

PSHE
1c. 4d.

English 1.
1a, b, c. 2a, c, d.
3a, c.

Did Leroy 'feel a little bit better' when he told Linda and mummy the naughty thing he had done? Did he cry when he admitted what he had eaten? Do you feel better and happier if you 'own up' and tell the truth? Did Linda and mummy give Leroy a hug and a kiss? Do you think that they felt sorry for Leroy?

226

Question 5 Do you think that Leroy will do the same thing again?

PSHE
1c. 2a.

Do you think that Leroy paid for what he had done? Do you think that eating a plum was enjoyable and did Leroy pay for it by feeling so bad? Do you think that Leroy would feel a plum was worth all the horrible and sad feelings that he experienced?

English 1.
1a, b, c. 2a, c, d.
3a, c.

Question 6 What did Leroy say he would do next time mummy gave them some plums and did Leroy feel better when they laughed?

Did he say he would give Linda his plum? Would this have been fair if Linda had liked the plums? When they all laughed do you think it might have made everyone feel better? Do you feel better when you laugh?

PSHE
1c. 2a. 4d.

Supplementary ideas

The teacher and children sit on the carpet. The teacher has the story of 'The Plums' written out on large strips of paper but the order is muddled. With the teacher's help the children put the story in its correct sequence. The teacher glues the story onto a large piece of paper in the correct sequence.

> One was for Linda and one was for Leroy.
> Leroy felt very sad.
> First mummy left two plums on a plate.
> Leroy told mummy and Linda what he had done.
> Mummy and Linda forgave him.
> Leroy ate both plums.

PSHE
1c. 4d.

English 1.
3b.

The teacher takes some plums into school. The teacher halves the plums demonstrating one half to the children. The children draw one half of the plum with its stone exposed.

The teacher takes out the stones and gives the children half a plum to eat. The teacher asks the children the following questions:

- How did they feel?

- Did they like eating the plum?

- Was it a good feeling?

PSHE
1a, c.

Art & Design.
1a.

The teacher gives each child a circle shape of paper divided equally into four. (One line vertically and one horizontally.) In each segment is written spring, summer, autumn or winter. The teacher tells the children to draw four plum trees. In the spring time the plum tree must be drawn in blossom. In summer the plum tree must be drawn with swelling plums. In the autumn the plum tree will have leaves of red, gold and brown. In the winter the tree will be a silhouette with no leaves. Ask the children if the tree is alive in all its seasons? What does it need in order to stay alive? If we poured weed killer on the tree would that be helpful or harmful to the tree? Should we pollute the environment? Would that be good for the tree? Is a cat alive? Is a car alive?

PSHE
2c.

Science 2.
I a.

Art & Design.
I a.

The teacher brings in various fruits. The children are given pieces of fruit to sample. How did they feel when they ate the fruit? Which fruit did they like best? She asks them to put up their hands if they liked banana best. The children are each given a small piece of paper just big enough for them to write on their name or their initials. The teacher repeats the exercise for each different kind of fruit. The teacher then collects the papers and uses them to make a block graph. Captions should read, for example, 'Ten people liked grapes best'. The pieces of paper should be colour coded. Perhaps yellow for banana, orange for oranges, green for grapes and purple for plums. The teacher could ask the children what is safe to eat from the following list:

PSHE
I a. 3f.

Maths 2.
I f.

bananas
berries from the garden
pills that the doctor gave to someone else
plums.

Worksheet instructions

"Look at the big picture. Can you see Leroy hiding in the bush? Why is he hiding? Do you think he is happy or sad? Do you think he is ashamed of what he has done? Do you think he feels guilty? What makes him feel better? Now look at the two pictures in the squares, one person is looking sad. Finish the pictures. Now colour in your pictures."

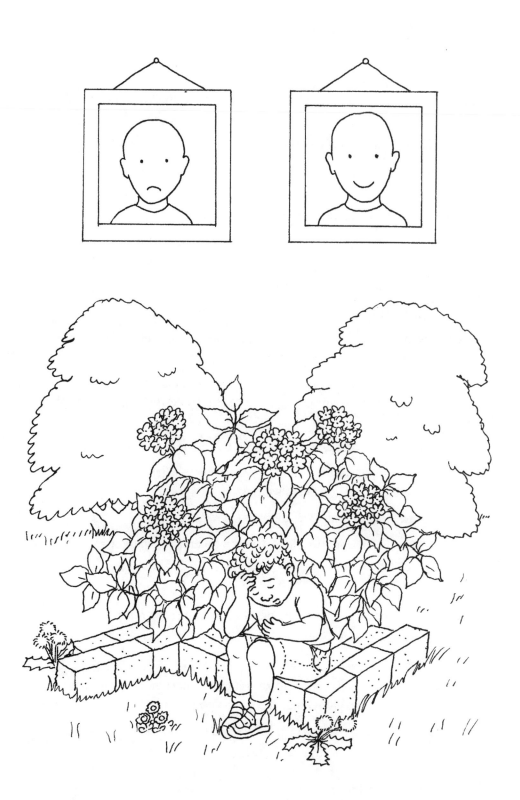

229 Lesson 22

The Plums

"Here are two plums," said Brenda to Leroy. "There is one for you and one for Linda."

"Please may I eat mine now?" asked Leroy.

"Yes, you may," replied his mummy and she went out into the garden to cut the grass.

Leroy ate his plum. It was very good and red and juicy.

Leroy looked out of the window. He could see his mummy. She was very busy.

Linda was not there. She was upstairs in her bedroom. She was playing her recorder. Leroy could hear her recorder tune.

Then the playing stopped. Linda was coming down the stairs.

Leroy looked at her plum, which was on the plate on the table. Leroy wanted Linda's plum. He wanted to eat another red juicy plum.

So he did. He had to eat it very quickly before Linda came into the room. He gobbled it up and then ran into the garden to find somewhere to hide the plum stone.

Linda did not know about the naughty thing that Leroy had done.

Their mummy was still very busy and Leroy was very worried. He felt upset and wished that he had not eaten Linda's plum.

He didn't know what to do and he didn't know what to say.

He tried to hide underneath the big hydrangea bush in the garden.

"What is the matter Leroy?" asked Linda when she saw where Leroy was hiding.

"Nothing," snapped Leroy. "Nothing, nothing, nothing!" He rushed back into the house, ran up the stairs and flung himself down on his bed.

Linda was puzzled.

"I don't think Leroy is well," she told her mummy when she came into the house after finishing the gardening. "Leroy has gone to bed."

Leroy was on his bed. He was asleep. He had all his clothes on.

Linda and mummy peeped round his bedroom door.

"Poor Leroy," said Linda.

"Poor Leroy," said mummy.

They crept downstairs again.

"We will be very kind to Leroy when he wakes up," said mummy. "He must be feeling unwell."

Linda and mummy kept very quiet. They did not want to disturb Leroy.

Leroy did not wake up. He stayed fast asleep on his bed until the next day.

The next day he woke up early. He wondered why he still had all his clothes on. Then he remembered about the naughty thing he had done. He remembered he had eaten Linda's plum. He wondered what Linda and mummy would say, but neither of them spoke about it. They were both very kind to Leroy.

All day they were very kind.

"Are you feeling better my good boy?" asked mummy.

"Would you like me to get your toys to play with?" asked Linda.

Leroy just shook his head. He tried to play with his toys, but he couldn't.

All day he tried to play, but he couldn't.

"Oh dear me!" said Brenda. "Something must be wrong with Leroy."

"It is," cried Leroy, "Something is very wrong. I ate Linda's plum and I am very, very sorry."

"So that is why you are ill, Leroy," said mummy, and she gave Leroy a big hug.

"Oh! Never mind," said Linda, "I didn't know about the plums."

She gave Leroy a friendly push then gave him a kiss.

Leroy felt a little bit better because he had told mummy and Linda about the naughty thing he had done, but he was still crying.

"Next time we have some plums to eat I will give mine to Linda," he sobbed.

"No! No! No! Leroy, don't do that," shouted Linda, "I don't like plums!"

Everyone laughed and laughed, and Leroy felt very much better.

Lesson 23: July

> **Story:** **The Goldfish**
> **Theme:** **Restoration and Recovery**

Synopsis

Baby Zoë wins a goldfish at the fair but she is too young to look after it and so Leroy and Linda become the proud owners. Life takes on a negative twist when the goldfish is obviously unwell. With the help of their daddy the twins help the goldfish to recover and it is re-housed in a tank with two new fish, rather than a goldfish bowl. Leroy and Linda's care and attention has saved the goldfish and they are responsible owners of their new pets.

Objectives

- To recognise what is right and wrong.

- To take part in discussion.

- To realise that living things have needs and that they have responsibilities to meet them.

- To maintain personal hygiene.

- To understand that families and friends care for one another.

- To set simple goals.

- To feel positive about themselves.

Preparing for the story

The teacher sits on a chair and the children gather around her on the carpet. The teacher has previously collected a series of items which can be used for restoration and recovery, for example medicine or pills (empty bottle), bandages, plasters, blanket, spectacles, holiday brochure, furniture or shoe polish and a hot water bottle. The teacher asks the children who, what and when would a person, animal or thing require and need the items listed above? Does everything need care and attention to recover?

PSHE
2a, e. 4d.

233

Read the story

After the above activity has been completed the teacher reads the story to the children.

Circle Time discussion

PSHE
1a.

English 1.
1a, b, c. 2a, c, d.
3a, c.

Question 1 How would you feel if you won something that you wanted very badly?

Would you be pleased and happy? Would you be sad? Would you 'dance for joy'?

PSHE
2a, e.

English 1.
1a, b, c. 2a, c, d.
3a, c.

Question 2 Leroy and Linda's mummy asked if Leroy and Linda were able to look after the goldfish. Do you think they could?

How did they show that they could look after the goldfish? Did they give it a name? Did they buy it some food with their spending money? Did they find some books from the library on goldfish care? Did they buy gravel and green plants for the goldfish? Did they help to make Zoë the goldfish well again when she was sick?

PSHE
2a, e.

English 1.
1a, b, c. 2a, c. d.
3a, c.

Science 2.
1a.

Question 3 Is a goldfish a living thing? Does it need care? Did Leroy and Linda give the goldfish what it needed?

Were Leroy and Linda responsible people when looking after their goldfish? Does a goldfish live? Does a screwdriver live?

PSHE
1a. 4d.

English 1.
1a, b, c. 2a, c, d.
3a, c.

Question 4 Was it right that Zoë was too young to look after the goldfish?

Was it right that Sali and Tim gave Leroy and Linda the goldfish? Can an 11-month-old baby girl care for a goldfish? Did Sali and Tim care for their neighbours?

PSHE
1a. 2a, e.

English 1.
1a, b, c. 2a, c, d.
3a, c.

Question 5 Could Leroy and Linda have decided to ignore the goldfish?

Why not? What would have happened then? Would it have been right and fair?

234

Question 6 How did Leroy, Linda and their daddy help the goldfish to recover?

PSHE
1a. 2a, e. 5a.

English 1.
1a, b, c. 2a, c, d.
3a, c.

What did they do to help? Was it kind and caring? Do you think the goldfish could have recovered without help? Do people and animals need extra help when they are ill? Is it right and fair to help them?

Supplementary ideas

The teacher explains to the children that Leroy and Linda had a goal. Their goal was to help the goldfish to recover. The teacher discusses with each child individually the goals that they will set themselves. For example it may be:

- Hanging up their coat.

- Tying their shoes laces.

- Learning to write their name.

- Learning a new letter of the alphabet and how to write that letter.

The teacher records the goals and at a later date checks to see if the children have attained that goal.

PSHE
1e.

The teacher or adult helper writes a sentence for the child to copy and complete. For example:

PSHE
5b.

English 3.
1d.

"Leroy and Linda were good at looking after goldfish. I am good at…"

The teacher tells the children that Linda and Leroy have been helping daddy to clean out the goldfish tank. The teacher asks the children to put up their hands if they know the next thing they should do:

should they clean their teeth
play with their toys or
wash their hands?

The teacher asks the children if they know of other times when they should wash their hands. They might suggest the following:

- Before they have a meal.

- After touching any animals.

- After going to the toilet.

- When their hands are dirty.

- If they have been playing outside.

- After using glue or paint.

Worksheet instructions

"Look at the worksheet with a fish in a bag, bowl and a tank. If you were a fish where would you choose to live? Colour the best place for a goldfish to live. In the rectangle at the bottom of the page draw your own fish and give it a name. Now look at the second worksheet. It is a picture of a goldfish. Decorate your goldfish."

(Provide some collage material and glue.)

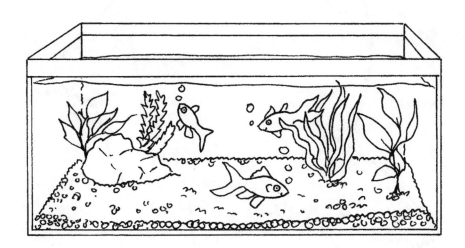

My fish is called...

The Goldfish

All the children in The Crescent knew that the fair was coming to the recreation ground. Leroy and Linda had been saving their spending money and couldn't wait for the day to arrive.

They were standing in Mr Allsort's shop with Josh, their daddy, when suddenly he said, "I'm sorry but I can't take you. I have work this weekend. It's a shame. I don't know how to make things better."

The children looked sad, and Josh didn't know what to do because he remembered how he had loved to go to the fair when he was a little boy.

Then a very nice thing happened.

"I will take them," said Tim, a neighbour and good friend of all the family. He had just come into the shop and had heard what they were talking about.

"Sali and I are taking Zoë, our little girl, to the fair on Saturday morning. Leroy and Linda are very welcome to come with us."

Leroy and Linda rushed over to Tim and gave him a big hug. They liked Tim.

"Yes, yes," they both shouted. "Yes, we want to come with you."

"Well," smiled Josh. "It looks as if you can go to the fair after all. I will come after work and meet you all by the entrance. Then Leroy and Linda can take me on a fairground ride."

Leroy and Linda were so happy that they skipped all the way home.

"Oh! I have just remembered," said Linda. "We have to do our jobs for mummy on Saturday. We have to change our beds and put all the dirty clothes in the laundry basket."

"Yes. That's our job," said Leroy. "But we can get up earlier, help mummy and still be ready by eleven o'clock. That's if we don't watch children's television."

"Good idea," said Linda. "I would rather go to the fair and I don't mind missing children's television this week."

Josh thought the children were being very thoughtful and kind. He told Brenda, their mummy, all about it.

She was pleased too. "If you help me a lot perhaps I will also have time to come to the fair."

"Wow!" laughed Linda. "What a good day it's going to be."

As promised Tim, Sali and Zoë came to their house at eleven o'clock. And as promised Leroy and Linda had helped their mummy with the jobs they were supposed to do and had even offered to help her with some more tidying up.

At the fair Tim took the children to their favourite ride while Sali stayed with baby Zoë. She was watching people throw ping-pong balls and trying to get them into goldfish bowls. If you threw a ball into a bowl you won a goldfish.

Zoë wanted to play too even though she was too young to understand what to do.

"Play. Play," she kept saying until Sali bought her a turn.

Zoë threw the first ball and it went completely the wrong way. It nearly hit someone on the head. Then there was a shout of delight and people started to clap. Zoë had thrown her second ball right into a goldfish bowl.

"She's won! She's won!" Sali giggled.

When Josh and Brenda arrived they were surprised to see Tim, Sali, baby Zoë, Leroy and Linda standing by the entrance gate and wearing big smiles. But they were even more surprised to see what Tim was holding in a plastic bag.

"Zoë's won a goldfish," explained Tim. "But she's too young to look after it. If it's all right with you I have said that Leroy and Linda can have it. I will go to the pet shop and buy a goldfish bowl."

"Can you look after it?" asked their mummy.

"Yes, we can," Leroy and Linda shouted.

"I think we will call it Zoë," said Leroy. "Linda and I agree it's the right name."

"And we've decided to buy it some food with our spending money," said Linda.

"You are good children. You are thinking like real grown-ups," said Brenda.

Each day Leroy and Linda learned more about goldfish care. They borrowed a book from the library, which Jenny their big sister read to them.

They bought some gravel and some green plants for the bowl and they learned that goldfish only need a little bit of food.

They followed all the rules carefully. They knew not to tap the glass bowl or put their hands in the water. Both these things could scare the goldfish.

All was going very well until a few weeks later when Zoë the goldfish started slipping over onto her side and sinking to the bottom of the bowl.

Leroy and Linda were very upset.

"Oh dear," said their daddy. "It's lost its balance. We will have to see if we can make it better."

Josh got a little plastic tank and poured in a small amount of water.

"We have to wait for a short time until the water has settled down. The water must not be too cold, and not too deep."

After a while Josh caught the fish in a small net and lowered it gently into the water in the new tank.

"That's not enough water for the fish to swim in," shouted Linda.

"The fish has got to get its balance back again," said Josh.

He made the water very shallow.

"If we're lucky the fish will get better. The water has to be just deep enough to keep the fish the right way up."

Each day Josh measured the water and each day he watched to see if the fish was swimming upright.

Then one day it started swimming properly. Josh put in a little more water and the next day a little more. After about three weeks the fish was swimming almost normally and the tank was nearly full of water.

"Now, I have a surprise for you, you clever goldfish," said Josh. "Go into the front room," he said to Linda and Leroy, "See if you notice anything different."

Leroy and Linda crept round the door. On a table in a corner of the room was a fish tank with two fish swimming happily in it. Inside the tank were water plants, lots of little stones and a big stone that they could rest behind.

"Here is your new home, Zoë goldfish," said Josh as he gently lowered the fish into the tank. "Meet your new friends."

"Let's call one Lee," said Leroy.

"And the other Lin," said Linda. "And we are going to look after them every day."

And they did.

Lesson 24: July

> **Story:** **The Plan**
> **Theme:** **Endings**

Synopsis

A year has passed and endings are inevitable but Leroy and Linda hatch their own plot to keep the students in The Crescent. Finally they understand that things alter and change and that all endings herald new beginnings.

Objectives

- To recognise what they like and dislike.

- To share their opinions on things that matter to them and explain their views.

- To recognise and name their feelings.

- To take part in discussion.

- To know that they belong to a class and a school.

- To recognise that there are safe things to do and things that are not so safe.

Preparing for the story

The teacher brings a globe into school. She shows it to the children. She asks whether the children can find the beginning or ending to the globe or does it simply merge into one. She discusses with the children about their opinions on beginnings and endings. When one thing ends does another begin? Can they think of when things began and ended for them?

PSHE
Ib. 2a.

Read the story

After the above activity has been completed the teacher reads the story to the children.

Circle Time discussion

PSHE
la.

English 1.
la, b, c. 2a, c, d.
3a, c.

Question 1 Was Leroy and Linda's plan a good plan? What were they trying to do?

Were Leroy and Linda trying to stop the students from going? Was this a good thing to do? Would it be fair to capture people?

PSHE
la, c. 3g.

English 1.
la, b, c. 2a, c, d.
3a, c.

Question 2 Why was Leroy and Linda's mummy worried?

Was Leroy and Linda's mummy worried because they were not safe locked up in a house on their own? What could be some of the dangers? Have you ever been worried? How did you feel?

Question 3 Next year will you be leaving the class that you are in?

PSHE
la. 2f.

English 1.
la, b, c. 2a, c. d.
3a, c.

What will happen after the holidays? Will you be leaving one class and starting another? Will the children in Year 6 be starting a new school? Can you remember being new? What did it feel like? Is it nice to be a member of your school? Are endings a little bit sad? Is a new beginning exciting? In September you might be moving on. Will you have a new start next time you move class?

PSHE
la.

English 1.
la, b, c. 2a, c, d.
3a, c.

Question 4 Has anybody ever gone away that you knew? How did you feel?

Did it make you sad if people went away? Is it nice to visit people who have moved away?

PSHE
lc. 3g.

English 1.
la, b, c. 2a, c, d.
3a, c.

Question 5 Did Josh really rescue the twins? Is it right for children to be left on their own?

Do you think Leroy and Linda would have felt scared if they had been left on their own at night? Did Leroy and Linda need their daddy and mummy? Would they have been safe on their own?

Question 6 What did Josh mean when he said, "all endings lead to new beginnings"?

Can you think of an ending and a new beginning? Tell the others what was important to you that had an ending and a new beginning. Can endings sometimes be sad, like when one pet dies - but then a new beginning might happen when a new pet comes to live with you. Changing classes and school, evening and morning - all are endings and new beginnings.

PSHE
1b. 2a.

English 1.
1a, b, c. 2a, c, d.
3a, c.

Supplementary ideas

The children discuss endings and beginnings with the teacher. They think about the endings and beginnings of going into a new class. How will they feel? The teacher gives each child a piece of paper folded into two. On one section the children draw a picture of the ending. Maybe the class they are in now and a new beginning, 'their new classroom.' Which teachers will be in their classrooms? Which furniture and equipment, toys etc., will be in their present and future classrooms?

PSHE
1b, c. 2a.

The teacher explains to the children that a new day begins when the sun rises in the morning. "We wake up and have our breakfast. We go to school. Every morning is a new beginning and every evening is an ending to that particular day but in the morning a new day has come and so it continues." The teacher asks the children to fold their arms if they think the following sentences are about the morning and put their hands on their heads if they think they are about the evening.

'I wake up and get dressed.'
'Then I get into my bed and go to sleep.'
'The moon goes down and the sun comes up.'
'I am read a bedtime story.'

The teacher discusses the following questions with the children. Can the children make morning and evenings a happy time? Can they do this by smiling and being happy? Is it good to accept beginnings and endings as part of life and the nature of things? Does how we behave make beginnings and endings happier or not so happy for other people? Do endings and new beginnings bring new experiences for everyone?

PSHE
1b. 4a.

Worksheet instructions

"You are going to draw your own picture story and tell your story to the class. Remember just draw pictures to tell your story. Your story starts by saying "First one day..." "Next..." and "Finally..." It ends by you saying "but that was not really the end because the next day..."

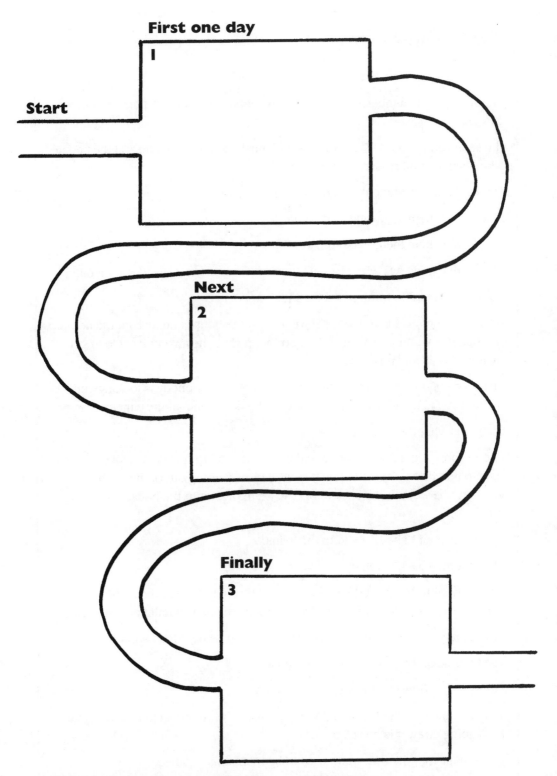

First one day

1

Start

Next

2

Finally

3

But that was not really the end because...

The Plan

The students at Number 9 The Crescent were having a leaving party in the garden.

It was the end of term. The students had finished all their exams. All the people who lived in The Crescent had been invited.

"I don't want the students to go away," said Leroy.

"I won't let them go away," said Linda.

"Shall we kidnap them?" asked Leroy.

"They are too big, we won't be able to catch them, Leroy," answered Linda.

So the twins had to think of a different idea.

After a few minutes Leroy said, "If we go into the house and lock all the doors the students won't be able to get in. So that means they won't be able to get their suitcases and go away."

"That's a good idea," said Linda. "Shall we wait until nobody is looking and then go inside the house? We will lock all the doors and all the windows."

So that is what the twins did.

After a short while Brenda wondered where her children were. It took her some time to find them. Then she saw two little faces peering out of the kitchen window. She went to the back door. She tried to get into the house. The door was locked.

"Open the door," she shouted to the twins.

They shouted back. "No!"

Brenda went to the front door. She shouted through the letterbox. She hammered on the door. She rang the doorbell. The twins would not let her in.

"What are you doing, Linda. What are you doing, Leroy?" Josh shouted.

The twins kept quiet. They would not answer.

"We want to come in," the students shouted.

This time the twins did answer. "You can't come in. We are going to stop you from going away. It is our plan."

"What happens when we want to go to bed?" Shama shouted.

"Go and sleep at our house," yelled Linda.

"Frisky will want something to eat. His food is in the house," shouted Stuart.

"We have some food in the fridge that your dog will like," Leroy answered.

"I want my electric shaver. Please let me in," Marcus pleaded.

"Borrow my dad's. He's got a good one," came the reply.

Just then there was a clanging noise. It made the twins jump. It was the little black kitten. It had come in through the cat flap.

"We will look after the cat," shouted Leroy. "We know where the fridge is. We will fill the dish with milk."

Nothing that anybody said would make the twins unlock the door.

"We have to get them out of the house," said Brenda. "They can't stay inside all by themselves. They are only small children. They could have an accident." She was worried.

"I will get my ladder," said Josh. "I will climb in through the bedroom window. The one at the front of the house is open."

"What are you doing here?" screamed Linda, when she saw her dad appear.

"How did you get in?" asked Leroy. "You can't come in. Go away."

"Well I am in," said Josh. He would not tell the twins how it had happened.

"Now you are our prisoner," Leroy told his dad. "We will lock you up."

"Yes, we will lock you up in this house. You can look after us. We can stay in here for days and days. The students will never be able to go away," said Linda. She was very happy.

"I don't know what to say to you two," Josh said. "When you finish school at the end of this term you will have a school party. Then you will leave school. Next year it will be a new start. It will be a new beginning. It is just the same for the students."

"But we are only little children. We have to go to school," the twins argued.

Josh unlocked the back door. He explained to everybody at the party why his children had locked the door. Everybody clapped. They were very pleased to see that the twins were safe.

All the students said that they would write to the twins to tell them how they were and what they were doing. They said that they would come back to The Crescent so see them from time to time.

"That was an interesting plan but I don't think it was a good idea to lock yourselves in. How did you think of it?" Josh asked his children later that evening.

"We didn't lock ourselves in. We locked people out," said Linda, rather indignantly.

"You tell us how you got into the house, and then we will tell you," said Leroy.

"That is my secret," said Josh. "I had to put an end to your plan but all endings lead to new beginnings."

The twins thought about that for a while. They didn't know what to say.

"I know, I know," shouted Leroy. "You got your ladder and climbed into the house."

"You are clever children," said Josh. "Perhaps you will be students one day." He tucked his children up into bed and kissed them and said, "Goodnight."

And very soon Leroy and Linda fell fast asleep.

Don't forget to visit our website for all our latest publications, news and reviews.

www.luckyduck.co.uk

New publications every year on our specialist topics:

- **Emotional Literacy**
- **Self-esteem**
- **Bullying**
- **Positive Behaviour Management**
- **Circle Time**
- **Anger Management**
- **Asperger's Syndrome**
- **Eating Disorders**